R.K. HAMLEN
East Jaffrey
N.H.

BRITISH LETTERS

ILLUSTRATIVE OF

CHARACTER AND SOCIAL LIFE

EDITED BY

EDWARD T. MASON

EDITOR OF "HUMOROUS MASTERPIECES," ETC.

NEW YORK & LONDON

G. P. PUTNAM'S SONS

The Knickerbocker Press

1888

Press of
G. P. PUTNAM'S SONS
New York

PREFACE.

The aim of this work is to present certain phases of life and character as described and exemplified by British letter-writers. While the search for materials has not been exhausttive, it has been reasonably thorough. The number of writers quoted is not particularly large; and that fact is a matter of indifference; for the end in view has not been to crowd the pages with distinguished names, but to insure the essential fitness of the selections—a fitness consisting in their special adaptation to the plan of the series.

The peculiar charm of letters—perhaps, also, their greatest value—is brought home to us when they are familiar, unstudied expressions of thought and feeling; when they betray no sense of a larger audience than the friends for whom alone they were written. The contents of these volumes do not uniformly maintain so high an excellence, but they exhibit many striking examples of it. Letters which are known to have been intended for publication,

or which were published by their writers, have
been excluded. To discriminate more closely
in selection was impracticable. It is a melancholy reflection, that all persons of marked
distinction must be haunted by a chilling consciousness that every scrap of their writing
may, sooner or later, be printed ; and their correspondence often betrays this consciousness.
Mrs. Carlyle, in writing to a friend, says :
"Geraldine . . . was so pleased with your
letter! 'My dear,' she said to me, 'how is it
that women who don't write books write always so much nicer letters than those who do?'
I told her it was, I supposed, because they did
not write in the valley of the shadow of their future biographers, but wrote what they had to say
frankly and naturally." Would that all letters
were so artlessly spontaneous as Mrs. Carlyle's!

It is hoped that the book may prove to be
something more than merely amusing; but
there has been a distinct intention to make it
agreeable. It aims to be a pleasant book ; and,
that it may be so, didactic and hortatory utter-
ances, and, more especially, accounts of afflic-
tion, have generally been avoided. A unique
and appalling volume might be made, composed

entirely of distressing letters. Sorrowful tales
of disaster; cries of grief; threatenings of tem-
poral and eternal woe, direful as any that ever
issued from the Vatican; gloomy, and sometimes ghastly introspections, which sound every
shoal and depth of morbid self-consciousness—
these, and other dispiriting things, are to be
found in British letters, and have been deemed
edifying. They certainly are not enlivening—
and none of them have been included. If men
need to be reminded that life has its tragic
side, there are many books admirably fitted to
supply that need, and the editor lacks ambition
to swell their number.

Chronological sequence has been disregarded,
except in the treatment of manners, and of
national traits, and in a few special instances
where there seemed to be value in the chronological arrangement. Elsewhere it proved to
be merely a hindrance, and was speedily dis-
carded. The letters have been grouped under
thirteen subject-headings, and have been carefully placed in such order as seemed most
logical and illustrative. If the design has been
tolerably well executed, some degree of order,
proportion, coherence, and definite purpose

will be discerned in the various sections of the book. It may fairly be claimed that they have not been prepared upon the happy-go-lucky plan of throwing together at random more or less congruous materials, ticketing them with a convenient title, and leaving the perplexed reader to determine their relevance to each other and to their common theme—to solve the futile anagram, "as wit and fortune will, or as the destinies decree."

Much has been omitted which would have found place in a larger work. Valuable letters, peculiarly suitable to the scope of this compilation, have been reluctantly abandoned, simply because there was no room for them. Abridgment has been used unsparingly; the plan of systematic arrangement under subject-headings made this absolutely necessary; but, in any case, the editorial privilege of omission would have been very freely used. There are comparatively few letters which would not be improved by abridgment. The perusal of numerous volumes of correspondence has begotten an ever-growing wonder that readers should be expected to find profit or amusement in what could have had value only at the time when it was written, and for the person to whom it was addressed. One reason for printing letters unabridged may be the solace derived by the editor who adopts that method; for he is thus spared many anxieties—delicate questions of taste, difficult questions of choice; he is freed from much responsibility, and enabled to run his course with delightful ease and rapidity.

None of Thackeray's letters to Mrs. Brookfield have been quoted. They have recently had such wide currency in two forms of publication, that it did not seem warrantable at the present time to present them again. Their importance demands this explanation; for in them the best qualities of letter-writing are exemplified: familiarity, which never offends against good taste; playfulness, unarmed with claws or teeth; keen perspicacity; above all, the frank unfolding of a beautiful and gracious character. They confirm all that we believed of that safe guide, wise philosopher, trusty friend, and come like a new series of the "Roundabout Papers" to enlarge our knowledge of the man. Nothing equal to them has appeared since Talfourd published the letters of Charles Lamb.

EDWARD T. MASON.

February 15, 1888.

CONTENTS.

AUTOBIOGRAPHIC SKETCHES.

MRS. THOMAS CARLYLE TO MRS. BRAID.

CHELSEA, May 22, 1863.

MY OWN BETTY * :—I am wearying for some news of you. I never could lay that proverb "No news is good news" sufficiently to heart. Whenever I am feeling poorly myself (and I should be almost ashamed to say how often that is the case), I fall to fancying that you are perhaps ill, and nobody to tell me of it, and I so far away! It is so stupid of Ann and Grace, who take so much fatigue on themselves, in visiting about in their "district," and attending all sorts of meetings, that they don't take a walk out of their district now and then to see how you are going on, and tell me when they write. Some news of Betty would make a letter from them infinitely more gratifying than any thing they can say about Dr. Candlish, and this and the other preacher and prayer; and would certainly inspire me with more Christian

* Betty was an old family servant.

feelings.   But, once for all, it is their way, and
there is no help for it.

O Betty! do you remember the little green
thing that I left in your care once while I was
over in Fife?   And when I returned you had
transplanted it into a yellow glass, which I have
on my toilet-table to this hour, keeping my
rings, etc., in it.   Well! I must surely have told
you long ago that the little thing, with two tiny
leaves, from my father's grave, had, after twelve
months in the garden at Chelsea, declared itself
a gooseberry-bush!   It has gone on flourishing,
in spite of want of air and of soil, and is now
the prettiest round bush, quite full of leaves.
I had several times asked our old gardener if
there is nothing one could do to get the bush
to bear, if it were only one gooseberry; but he
treated the case as hopeless.   " A poor wild
thing.   No ; if you want to have gooseberries,
ma'am, better get a proper gooseberry-bush in
its place! "   The old Goth!   He can't be made
to understand that things can have any value
but just their garden value.   He once, in spite
of all I could beg and direct, rooted out a nettle
I had brought from Crawford Churchyard, and
with infinite pains got to take root and flourish.

But, I was going to tell you, one day Lizzy, my youngest maid, came running in from the garden to ask me had I seen the three little gooseberries on the gooseberry-bush? I rushed out, as excited as a child, to look at them. And there they were—three little gooseberries, sure enough! And immediately I had settled it in my mind to send you one of them in a letter when full grown. But, alas! whether it was through too much staring at them, or too much east wind, or through mere delicacy in "the poor wild thing," I can't tell; only the result, that the three bits of gooseberries, instead of growing larger, grew every day less, till they reached the smallness of pin-heads, and then dropped on the ground! I could have cried when the last one went. . . .

———

MRS. THOMAS CARLYLE TO MRS. MARY RUSSELL.

CHELSEA, August 30, 1861.

Darling! I want to hear about you; and that is lucky for you, if you be at all wanting to hear about me! For I'll be hanged if mere unassisted sense of duty, and that sort of thing, could nerve me to sit down and write a letter in these days, when it takes pretty well all the

sense and strength I have left to keep myself
soul and body together, doing the thing forced
into my hands to do, and answering when I
am spoken to. A nice woman I am! But I
know you have been in such depths yourself
occasionally, and will have sympathy with me,
instead of being contemptuous or angry, as
your strong-minded, able-bodied women would
be ; and accordingly strong-minded, able-bodied
women are my aversion, and I run out of the
road of one as I would from a mad cow. The
fact is, had there been nobody in the world to
consider except myself, I ought to have " carried out " that project I had set my heart on of
streaming off by myself to Holm Hill, and taking a life-bath, as it were, in my quasi-
natural air, in the scene of old affections, not
all past and gone, but some still there as alive
and warm, thank God! as ever, and only the
dearer for being mixed up with those that are
dead and gone. . . .

JAMES BOSWELL TO W. J. TEMPLE.

LONDON, May 14, 1768.

 . . . I am really the *great man* now. I have
had David Hume, in the forenoon, and Mr. John-

son, in the afternoon, of the same day, visiting
me. Sir John Pringle, Dr. Franklin, and some
more company, dined with me to-day; and Mr.
Johnson and General Oglethorpe one day, Mr.
Garrick alone another, and David Hume and
some more *literati* dine with me next week. I
give admirable dinners and good claret; and the
moment I go abroad again, which will be in a
day or two, I set up my chariot. This is enjoying the fruit of my labors, and appearing like
the friend of Paoli. By the bye, the Earl of
Pembroke and Captain Meadows are just set-
ting out for Corsica, and I have the honor of
introducing them by a letter to the General.
David Hume came on purpose, the other day,
to tell me that the Duke of Bedford was very
fond of my book,* and had recommended it to
the Duchess. David is really amiable: I always
regret to him his unlucky principles, and he
smiles at my faith; but I have a hope which he
has not, or pretends not to have. So who has
the best of it, my reverend friend? David is
going to give us two more volumes of History,
down to George II. . . .

* His " Account of Corsica," then recently published.

JAMES BOSWELL TO W. J. TEMPLE.

EDINBURGH, June 6, 1775.

Believe me, your excellent letter of the 27th
of May, which I received last night, after my
coming home fatigued, after seeing a review,
was exceedingly refreshing to me; nay, it
elevated my mind higher than I can well express to so intimate a friend; for it is most
certain that all expressions of compliment or
kindness between such friends as we are ought
to be superfluous.   General Paoli told me
lately that his brother was ill; he consulted
physicians in London, and informed him of
what they said; but he never once put in
words that he was sorry or affectionately concerned, for he thought that would be quite unnecessary : he was so obliging as to apply this
remark to me : " I need not tell you," said he,
" that every thing in my power is at your disposal."   For the last fortnight that I was in
London, since I saw you, I lay at his house,
and had the command of his coach.   My lodgings in Gerrard Street were taken by a gentleman for a longer time than I could stay; so it
was obliging my landlord to quit them, and all
cards and messages of every kind were taken in

there for me. I felt more dignity when I had several servants at my devotion, a large apartment, and the convenience and state of the coach. I recollected that *this dignity in London* was honorably acquired by my travels abroad, and my pen after I came home, so I could enjoy it with my own approbation, and in the extent and multiplicity of the metropolis other people had not even the materials for finding fault, as my situation was not particularly known. . . .

————

SAMUEL JOHNSON TO LORD CHESTERFIELD.

February 7, 1775.

I have been lately informed by the proprietor of *The World* that two papers, in which my Dictionary is recommended to the public, were written by your lordship. To be so distinguished is an honor which, being very little accustomed to favors from the great, I know not well how to receive, or in what terms to acknowledge.

When, upon some slight encouragement, I first visited your lordship, I was overpowered, like the rest of mankind, by the enchantment of your address, and could not forbear to wish

that I might boast myself *le vainqueur du vainqueur de la terre ;* that I might obtain that regard for which I saw the world contending;
but I found my attendance so little encouraged
that neither pride nor modesty would suffer me
to continue it. When I had once addressed
your lordship in public, I had exhausted all the
art of pleasing which a retired and uncourtly
scholar can possess. I had done all that I
could, and no man is well pleased to have his
all neglected, be it ever so little.

Seven years, my lord, have now passed since I
waited in your outward rooms, or was repulsed
from your door; during which time I have been
pushing on my work through difficulties of
which it is useless to complain, and have
brought it, at last, to the verge of publication,
without one act of assistance, one word of encouragement, or one smile of favor. Such
treatment I did not expect, for I never had a
patron before.

The shepherd in Virgil grew at last acquainted with Love, and found him a native
of the rocks.

Is not a patron, my lord, one who looks with
unconcern on a man struggling for life in the
water, and, when he has reached ground, en-

cumbers him with help? The notice which you have been pleased to take of my labors, had it been early, had been kind; but it has been delayed till I am indifferent, and cannot enjoy it; till I am solitary, and cannot impart it; till I am known, and do not want it. I hope it is no very cynical asperity not to confess obligations where no benefit has been received, or to be unwilling that the public should consider me as owing that to a patron, which Providence has enabled me to do for myself.

Having carried on my work thus far with so little obligation to any favorer of learning, I shall not be disappointed, though I should conclude it, if less be possible, with less; for I have been long wakened from that dream of hope, in which I once boasted myself with so much exultation, my lord,

Your lordship's most humble, most obedient servant, ———— SAM. JOHNSON.

OLIVER GOLDSMITH TO DANIEL HODSON.

TEMPLE EXCHANGE COFFEE-HOUSE,
NEAR TEMPLE BAR,
December 27, 1757.

. . . You may easily imagine what difficulties I had to encounter, left as I was without friends, recommendations, money, or impudence; and that in a country where being born an Irishman was sufficient to keep me unemployed. Many in such circumstances would have had recourse to the friar's cord or the suicide's halter. But with all my follies, I had principle to resist the one, and resolution to combat the other.

I suppose you desire to know my present situation. As there is nothing in it at which I should blush, or which mankind could censure, I see no reason for making it a secret; in short, by a very little practice as a physician and a very little reputation as a poet, I make a shift to live. . . . Upon hearing I write, no doubt you imagine I starve; and the name of an author naturally reminds you of a garret. In this particular I do not think proper to un-deceive my friends. But whether I eat or starve, live in a first floor or four pairs of stairs high, I still remember them with ardor, nay, my very country comes in for a share of my af-fection. Unaccountable fondness for country, this *maladie du pays*, as the French call it! Un-accountable that he should still have an affection for a place who never received, when in it, above common civility; who never brought any thing out of it except his brogue and his blunders. Surely my affection is equally ridiculous with the Scotchman's, who refused to be cured of the itch, because it made him unco' thoughtful of his wife and bonny Inverary. . . .

I confess I carry this spirit sometimes to the souring the pleasures I at present possess. If I go to the opera where Signora Columba pours out all the mazes of melody, I sit and sigh for Lishoy fireside, and Johnny Armstrong's Last Good-Night, from Peggy Golden. If I climb Flamstead Hill, than where nature never exhibited a more magnificent prospect—I confess it fine—but then, I had rather be placed on the little mount before Lishoy gate, and there take in, to me, the most pleasing horizon in nature. . . .

OLIVER GOLDSMITH TO MRS. JANE LAWDER.

TEMPLE EXCHANGE COFFEE-HOUSE,
TEMPLE BAR,
August 15, 1758.

. . . It is probable you may one of these days see me turned into a perfect hunks, and as dark and intricate as a mouse-hole. I have already given my landlady orders for an entire reform in the state of my finances. I declaim against hot suppers, drink less sugar in my tea, and

check my grate with brick-bats. Instead of
hanging my room with pictures, I intend to
adorn it with maxims of frugality. Those will
make pretty furniture enough, and won't be a
bit too expensive; for I shall draw them all out
with my own hands, and my landlady's daughter shall frame them with the parings of my
black waistcoat. Each maxim is to be inscribed
on a sheet of clean paper, and wrote with my
best pen, of which the following will serve as a
specimen: "Look sharp"; "Mind the main
chance"; "Money is money now"; "If you
have a thousand pounds, you can put your
hands by your sides and say you are worth a
thousand pounds every day of the year";
"Take a farthing from a hundred, and it will be
a hundred no longer." Thus, which way soever
I turn my eyes they are sure to meet one of
those friendly monitors; and as we are told of
an actor who hung his room round with look-
ing-glass to correct the defects of his person,
my apartment shall be furnished in a peculiar
manner, to correct the errors of my mind.

Faith! Madam, I heartily wish to be rich, if
it were only for this reason—to say without a
blush how much I esteem you; but alas! I have

many a fatigue to encounter before that happy
time comes, when your poor old simple friend
may again give a loose to the luxuriance of
his nature, sitting by Kilmore fireside, recount
the various adventures of a hard-fought life,
laugh over the follies of the day, join his flute
to your harpsichord, and forget that ever he
starved in those streets where Butler and Otway
starved bofere him. . . .

WALTER SAVAGE LANDOR TO ROBERT SOUTHEY.

FLORENCE, April 11, 1825.

Taylor's first villainy in making me disappoint the person with whom I had agreed for
the pictures instigated me to throw my fourth
volume, in its imperfect state, into the fire, and
and has cost me nine tenths of my fame as a
writer. His next villainy will entail perhaps a
Chancery suit on my children,—for at its commencement I blow my brains out. Mr. Hazlitt,
Mr. Leigh Hunt, Lord Dillon, Mr. Brown, and
some other authors of various kinds, have been
made acquainted, one from another, with this
whole affair, and they speak of it as a thing
unprecedented. It is well that I rewrote the
" Tiberius and Vipsania " before Taylor gave

me a fresh proof of his intolerable roguery.
This cures me for ever, if I live, of writing
what could be published; and I will take good
care that my son shall not suffer in the same
way. Not a line of any kind will I leave behind
me. My children shall be carefully warned
against literature. To fence, to swim, to speak
French, are the most they shall learn.

———

ROBERT SOUTHEY TO GROSVENOR C. BEDFORD.

BRISTOL, April 3, 1803.

. . . I love old houses best, for the sake of the
odd closets and cupboards, and good thick walls
that don't let the wind blow in, and little out-
of-the-way polyangular rooms, with great beams
running across the ceiling—old heart of oak,
that has outlasted half a score of generations;
and chimney-pieces with the date of the year
carved above them, and huge fire-places that
warmed the shins of Englishmen before the
house of Hanover came over. The most delightful associations that ever made me feel,
and think, and fall a-dreaming, are excited by
old buildings—not absolute ruins, but in a state
of decline. Even the clipped yews interest me;
and if I found one in any garden that should

become mine, in the shape of a peacock, I should be as proud to keep his tail well spread as the man who first carved him. In truth, I am more disposed to connect myself by sympathy with the ages which are past, and by hope with those that are to come, than to vex and irritate myself by any lively interest about the existing generation. . . .

ROBERT SOUTHEY TO SAMUEL TAYLOR COLERIDGE.

GRETA HALL, March 12, 1804.

. . . You would rejoice with me were you now at Keswick, at the tidings that a box of books is safely harbored in the Mersey, so that for the next fortnight I shall be more interested in the news of Fletcher * than of Bonaparte. It contains some duplicates of the lost cargo ; among them, the collection of the old Spanish poems, in which is a metrical romance upon the Cid. I shall sometimes want you for a Gothic etymology. Talk of the happiness of getting a great prize in the lottery! What is that to the opening a box of books! The joy upon lifting up the cover must be something like what we shall feel when Peter the Porter opens the door

* A Keswick carrier.

up-stairs, and says, "Please to walk in, sir." That I shall never be paid for my labor is tolerably certain; but if any one should offer me £10,000 to forego that labor, I should bid him and his money to go to the devil, for twice the sum could not purchase me half the enjoyment. It will be a great delight to me in the next world to take a fly and visit these old worthies, who are my only society here, and to tell them what excellent company I found them here at the lakes of Cumberland, two centuries after they had been dead and turned to dust. In plain truth, I exist more among the dead than the living, and think more about them, and, perhaps, feel more about them. . . .

ROBERT SOUTHEY TO NICHOLAS LIGHTFOOT.

KESWICK, April 24, 1807.

. . . Your last letter is fourteen months old, and they may have brought forth so many changes that I almost fear to ask for my godchild, Fanny. During that time I have had a son born into the world, and baptized into the Church by the name of Herbert, who is now six months old, and bids fair to be as noisy a fellow as his father—which is saying something;

for be it known that I am quite as noisy as ever I was, and should take as much delight as ever in showering stones through the hole of the staircase against your room door, and hearing with what good earnest " you fool ! " was vociferated in indignation against me in return. O dear Lightfoot, what a blessing it is to have a boy's heart ! it is as great a blessing in carrying one through this world as to have a child's spirit will be in fitting us for the next. . . .

I sometimes think with wonder how few acquaintances I made at Oxford; except yourself and Burnett, not one whom I should feel any real pleasure in meeting. Of all the months in my life (happily they did not amount to years), those which were passed at Oxford were the most unprofitable. What Greek I took there I literally left there, and could not help losing; and all I learned was a little swimming (very little, the worse luck) and a little boating, which is greatly improved, now that I have a boat of my own upon this delightful lake. I never remember to have dreamed of Oxford— a sure proof how little it entered into my moral being; of school, on the contrary, I dream perpetually. . . .

Vol. I.

ROBERT SOUTHEY TO GROSVENOR C. BEDFORD.

KESWICK, November 17, 1808.

. . . Let not Gifford suppose me a trouble-some man to deal with, pertinacious about trifles, or standing upon punctilios of authorship. No, Grosvenor, I am a quiet, patient, easy-going hack of the mule breed; regular as clock-work in my pace, sure-footed, bearing the burden which is laid on me, and only obstinate in choosing my own path. If Gifford could see me by this fireside, where, like Nicodemus, one candle suffices me in a large room, he would see a man in a coat "still more threadbare than his own" when he wrote his "Imitation," work-ing hard and getting little—a bare maintenance, and hardly that; writing poems and history for posterity, with his whole heart and soul; one daily progressive in learning, not so learned as he is poor, and not so poor as proud, not so proud as happy. Grosvenor, there is not a lighter-hearted nor a happier man on the face of this wide world.

Your godson thinks that I have nothing to do but to play with him, and anybody who saw what reason he has for his opinion would be disposed to agree with him. I wish you could see my beautiful boy !

WILLIAM WORDSWORTH TO SIR GEORGE BEAUMONT.

GRASSMERE, June 3, 1805.

I write you from the moss-hut at the top of my orchard, the sun just sinking behind the hills in front of the entrance, and his light falling upon the green moss of the side opposite me. A linnet is singing in the tree above, and the children of some of our neighbors, who have been to-day little John's visitors, are playing below, equally noisy and happy. The green fields in the level area of the vale, and part of the lake, lie before me in quietness. I have just been reading two newspapers, full of factious brawls about Lord Melville and his delinquencies, ravage of the French in the West Indies, victories of the English in the East, fleets of ours roaming the sea in search of enemies whom they cannot find, etc., etc., etc.; and I have asked myself more than once lately, if my affections can be in the right place, caring as I do so little about what the world seems to care so much for. All this seems to me, " a tale told by an idiot, full of sound and fury, signifying nothing." It is pleasant in such a mood to turn one's thoughts to a good man and a dear friend. I have, therefore, taken up the pen to write to you. . . .

I have the pleasure to say that I finished my poem * about a fortnight ago. I had looked forward to the day as a most happy one; and I was indeed grateful to God for giving me life to complete the work, such as it is. But it was not a happy day for me; I was dejected on many accounts: when I looked back upon the performance, it seemed to have a dead weight about it,—the reality so far short of the expectation. It was the first long labor that I had finished; and the doubt whether I should ever live to write "The Recluse," and the sense which I had of this poem being so far below what I seemed capable of executing, depressed me much; above all, many heavy thoughts of my poor departed brother hung upon me, the joy which I should have had in showing him the manuscript, and a thousand other vain fancies and dreams. I have spoken of this, because it was a state of feeling new to me, the occasion being new. This work may be considered as a sort of *portico* to "The Recluse," part of the same building, which I hope to be able, erelong, to begin with in earnest; and if I am permitted to bring it to a conclusion, and to write, fur-

* " The Prelude."

ther, a narrative poem of the epic kind, I shall consider the task of my life as over. I ought to add, that I have the satisfaction of finding the present poem not quite of so alarming a length as I apprehended. . . .

WILLIAM WORDSWORTH TO LADY BEAUMONT.

COLEORTON, May 21, 1807.

Though I am to see you so soon, I cannot but write a word or two to thank you for the interest you take in my poems, as evinced by your solicitude about their immediate reception. I write partly to thank you for this and to express the pleasure it has given me, and partly to remove any uneasiness from your mind which the disappointments you sometimes meet with in this labor of love may occasion. I see that you have many battles to fight for me; more than, in the ardor and confidence of your pure and elevated mind, you had ever thought of being summoned to; but be assured that this opposition is nothing more than what I distinctly foresaw that you and my other friends would have to encounter. I say this, not to give myself credit for an eye of prophecy, but to allay any vexatious thoughts on my

account which this opposition may have produced in you.

It is impossible that any expectations can be
lower than mine concerning the immediate effect of this little work upon what is called the
public. I do not here take into consideration
the envy and malevolence, and all the bad passions which always stand in the way of a work
of any merit from a living poet, but merely
think of the pure, absolute, honest ignorance in
which all worldlings of every rank and situation
must be enveloped with respect to the thoughts,
feelings, and images on which the life of my
poems depends. The things which I have taken,
whether from within or without—what have
they to do with routs, dinners, morning calls,
hurry from door to door, from street to street,
on foot or in carriage; with Mr. Pitt or Mr.
Fox, Mr. Paul or Sir Francis Burdette; the
Westminster election or the borough of Honi-
ton? In a word—for I cannot stop to make
my way through the hurry of images that present
themselves to me—what have they to do with
endless talking about things nobody cares any
thing for, except as far as their own vanity is concerned, and this with persons they care nothing

for, but as their vanity or *selfishness* is concerned? What have they to do (to say all at
once) with a life without love? In such a life
there can be no thought; for we have no
thought (save thoughts of pain) but as far as
we have love and admiration.

It is an awful truth that there neither is, nor
can be, any genuine enjoyment of poetry among
nineteen out of twenty of those persons who
live, or wish to live, in the broad light of the
world—among those who either are, or are striving to make themselves, people of consideration
in society. This is a truth, and an awful one,
because to be incapable of a feeling of poetry,
in my sense of the word, is to be without love
of human nature and reverence for God.

Upon this I shall insist elsewhere; at present
let me confine myself to my object, which is to
make you, my dear friend, as easy-hearted as
myself with respect to these poems. Trouble
not yourself upon their present reception; of
what moment is that compared with what I
trust is their destiny—to console the afflicted;
to add sunshine to daylight, by making the
happy happier; to teach the young and the
gracious of every age to see, to think, and feel;

and therefore to become more actively and securely virtuous; this is their office, which I trust they will faithfully perform long after we (that is, all that is mortal of us) are mouldered in our graves. . . .

My letter (as this second sheet which I am obliged to take admonishes me) is growing to an enormous length; and yet, saving that I have expressed my calm confidence that these poems will live, I have said nothing which has a particular application to the object of it, which was to remove all disquiet from your mind on account of the condemnation they may at present incur from that portion of my contemporaries who are called the public. I am sure, my dear Lady Beaumont, if you attach any importance to it, it can only be from an apprehension that it may affect me, upon which I have already set you at ease; or from a fear that this present blame is ominous of their future or final destiny. If this be the case, your tenderness for me betrays you. Be assured that the decision of these persons has nothing to do with the question; they are altogether incompetent judges. These people, in the senseless hurry of their lives, do not *read* books;

they merely snatch a glance at them, that they may talk about them. And even if this were not so, never forget what I believe was observed to you by Coleridge, that every great and original writer, in proportion as he is great or original, must himself create the taste by which he is to be relished. He must teach the art by which he is to be seen; this, in a certain degree, even to all persons, however wise and pure may be their lives, and however unvitiated their taste. But for those who dip into books in order to give an opinion of them, or talk about them to take up an opinion—for this multitude of unhappy, and misguided, and misguiding beings, an entire regeneration must be produced; and if this be possible, it must be a work *of time.* To conclude, my ears are stone-dead to this idle buzz, and my flesh as insensible as iron to these petty stings; and after what I have said I am sure yours will be the same. I doubt not that you will share with me an invincible confidence that my writings (and among them these little poems) will coöperate with the benign tendencies in human nature and society, wherever found; and that they will in their degree be efficacious in making men wiser, better, and happier. Farewell. . . .

THOMAS DE QUINCEY TO HIS DAUGHTER, MRS.
MARGARET CRAIG.

Thursday, June 10, 1847.

I am rather disturbed that neither M. nor F.
nor E. has found a moment for writing to me.
Yet perhaps it was not easy.   For I know very
seriously, and have often remarked, how difficult it is to find a spare moment for some
things in the very longest day, which lasts, you
know, twenty-four hours, though by the way it
strikes one as odd that the shortest lasts quite as
many.   I have been suffering greatly myself for
ten days, the cause being, in part, some out-
rageous heat that the fussy atmosphere put
itself into about the beginning of this month—
but what *for* nobody can understand.   Heat
always untunes the harp of my nervous system,
and, O heavens! how electric it is!   But,
after all, what makes me so susceptible of such
undulations in this capricious air, and compels
me to sympathize with all the uproars and *miffs*,
towering passions, or gloomy sulks of the atmosphere, is the old eternal ground, viz., that I am
famished.   O what ages it is since I dined!
On what great day of jubilee is it that Fate
hides, under the thickest of table-cloths, a din-

ner for *me?* Yet it is a certain, undeniable
truth, which this personal famine has revealed
to me, that most people on this terraqueous
globe eat too much. Which it is, and nothing
else, that makes them stupid, as also unphilo-
sophic. To be a philosopher it is absolutely
necessary to be famished. My intellect is far
too electric in its speed, and its growth of flying armies of thoughts eternally new. I could
spare enough to fit out a nation. This secret
lies—not, observe, in my hair; cutting off *that*
does no harm; it lies in my want of dinner, as
also of breakfast and supper. Being famished,
I shall show this world of ours in the next five
years something that it never saw before. But
if I had a regular dinner, I should sink into
the general stupidity of my beloved human
brethren.

JOHN KEATS TO JOHN HAMILTON REYNOLDS.

TEIGNMOUTH, April 9, 1818.

Since you all agree that the thing* is bad, it
must be so, though I am not aware there is
any thing like Hunt in it (and if there is, it is
my natural way, and I have something in common with Hunt). Look it over again, and ex-

* His first preface to "Endymion."

amine into the motives, the seeds, from which
any one sentence sprung.

I have not the slightest feel of humility towards the public, or to any thing in existence
but the Eternal Being, the Principle of Beauty,
and the Memory of great Men.   When I am
writing for myself, for the mere sake of the
moment's enjoyment, perhaps nature has its
course with me ; but a Preface is written to
the public—a thing I cannot help looking upon
as an enemy, and which I cannot address without feelings of hostility.   If I write a Preface
in a supple or subdued style, it will not be in
character with me as a public speaker.

I would be subdued before my friends, and
thank them for subduing me; but among mul-
titudes of men I have no feel of stooping ; I
hate the idea of humility to them.

I never wrote one single line of poetry with
the least shadow of public thought.

Forgive me for vexing you and making a
Trojan horse of such a trifle, both with respect
to the matter in question and myself; but it
eases me to tell you : I could not live without
the love of my friends ; I would jump down
Ætna for any great public good, but I hate a

mawkish popularity. I cannot be subdued before them. My glory would be to daunt and
dazzle the thousand jabberers about pictures
and books. . . .　　———

JOHN KEATS TO JOHN TAYLOR.

TEIGNMOUTH, April 27, 1818.

. . . I was proposing to travel over the North
this summer. There is but one thing to prevent
me. I know nothing, I have read nothing, and
I mean to follow Solomon's directions; "Get
learning; get understanding." I find earlier
days are gone by; I find that I can have no
enjoyment in the world but continual drinking
of knowledge; I find there is no worthy pur-
suit but the idea of doing some good to the
world. Some do it with their society; some
with their wit; some with their benevolence;
some with a sort of power of conferring pleasure and good humor on all they meet, and in a
thousand ways, all dutiful to the command of
great Nature. There is but one way for me.
The road lies through application, study, and
thought. I will pursue it, and for that end
purpose retiring for some years. I have been
hovering for some time between an exquisite

sense of the luxurious, and a love for philosophy. Were I calculated for the former, I should be glad.   But as I am not, I shall turn all my soul to the latter. . . .   _____

JOHN KEATS TO JAMES AUGUSTUS HESSEY.

October 9, 1818.

. . . Praise or blame has but a momentary effect on the man whose love of beauty in the abstract makes him a severe critic on his own works.   My own domestic criticism has given me pain without comparison beyond what *Blackwood* or the *Quarterly* could possibly inflict, and also when I feel I am right, no external praise can give me such a glow as my own solitary reperception and ratification of what is fine.   J. S. is perfectly right in regard to the "slip-shod 'Endymion.'"   That it is so is no fault of mine.   No! though it may sound a little paradoxical, it is as good as I had power to make it by myself.   Had I been nervous about its being a perfect piece, and with that view asked advice, and trembled over every page, it would not have been written; for it is not in my nature to fumble.   I will write independently.   I have written independently *with-*

out judgment. I may write independently and
with judgment, hereafter. The Genius of Poetry
must work out its own salvation in a man. It
cannot be matured by law and precept, but by
sensation and watchfulness in itself. That
which is creative must create itself. In "Endymion" I leaped headlong into the sea, and
thereby have become better acquainted with
the soundings, the quicksands, and the rocks
than if I had stayed upon the green shore and
piped a silly pipe, and took tea and comfortable
advice. I was never afraid of failure; for I
would sooner fail than not be among the
greatest. . . .

JOHN KEATS TO WILLIAM REYNOLDS.

WINCHESTER, August 25, 1819.

By this post I write to Rice, who will tell
you why we have left Shanklin, and how we
like the place. I have indeed scarcely any
thing else to say, leading so monotonous a life,
unless I was to give you a history of sensations
and day nightmares. You would not find me
at all unhappy in it, as all my thoughts and
feelings, which are of the selfish nature, home
speculations, every day continue to make me

more iron. I am convinced more and more, every day, that fine writing is, next to fine doing, the top thing in the world ; the " Paradise Lost " becomes a greater wonder. The more I know what my diligence may in time probably effect, the more does my heart distend with pride and obstinacy. I feel it in my power to become a popular·writer. I feel it in my power to refuse the poisonous suffrage of a public. My own being, which I know to be, becomes of more consequence to me than the crowds of shadows in the shape of men and women that inhabit a kingdom. The soul is a world of itself, and has enough to do in its own home. Those whom I know already and who have grown as it were a part of myself, I could not do without ; but for the rest of mankind, they are as much a dream to me as Milton's " Hierarchies." I think if I had a free and healthy and lasting organization of heart, and lungs as strong as an ox, so as to be able to bear unhurt the shock of extreme thought and sensation without weariness, I could pass my life very nearly alone, though it should last eighty years. But I feel my body too weak to support me to this height ; I am obliged continually to check myself, and be nothing.

It would be vain for me to endeavor after a more reasonable manner of writing to you. I have nothing to speak of but myself, and what can I say but what I feel? If you should have any reason to regret this state of excitement in me, I will turn the tide of your feelings in the right channel, by mentioning that it is the only state for the best sort of poetry—that is all I care for, all I live for. Forgive me for not filling up the whole sheet; letters become so irksome to me, that the next time I leave London I shall petition them all to be spared me. To give me credit for constancy, and at the same time waive letter-writing, will be the highest indulgence I can think of.

<hr />

LEIGH HUNT TO MR. IVES.

SURREY JAIL, February 5, 1813.

Mr. Leigh Hunt presents his compliments to Mr. Ives, and puts down his wishes upon paper as requested.

His first and greatest wish, then, is to be allowed to have his wife and children living with him in the prison. It is to be observed, that his is a new case within these walls; and not only so, but that his habits have always been of the most domestic kind, that he has not been

Vol. I.

accustomed to be from home a day long, and
that he is subject, particularly at nighttime, to
violent attacks of illness, accompanied by pal-
pitations of the heart and other nervous affections, which render a companion not only much
wanted, but sometimes hardly to be dispensed
with. His state of health is bad at the present
moment, as anybody may see ; not so bad indeed as it has been, and he wishes to make no
parade of it ; but quite bad enough to make
him feel tenfold all the wants of his situation,
and to render it absolutely necessary that his
greatest comforts should not all be taken away.
If it would take time, however, to consider this
request, his next wish is that his wife and children be allowed to be with him in the daytime.
His happiness is bound up in them, and he shall
say no more on this subject, except that a total
separation in respect to abode would be almost
as bad to him as tearing his body asunder.

His third and last request is, that his friends
be allowed to come up to his room during the
daytime ; and if this permission be given, he
will give his word that it shall not be abused.
His physician has often declared that society is
necessary to his health ; but though he has been

used to every comfort that domestic and social happiness can bestow, he is content with as little as possible, and provided his just wish be granted, could make almost any sacrifice.

This is all he has to say on the subject, and all with which he should ever trouble anybody. The hope of living in Mr. Ives's house he has given up ; many privations, of course, he is prepared to endure ; with the other regulations of the prison he has no wish to interfere ; and from what little has already been seen of him in this place, he believes that every credit will be given him for conducting himself in a reasonable and gentlemanly manner ; for as he is a stubborn enemy of what is wrong, so is he one of the quietest and most considerate friends of what is right. He has many private friends who would do their utmost for him ; and his character, he believes, has procured him some public ones of the highest description, who would leave no means untaken for bettering his condition, but he would willingly leave his comforts to those about him. To conclude, he is prepared to suffer all extremities rather than do himself dishonor ; but it is no dishonor to have the feelings of a husband and a father ;

and till he is dead to them and to every thing else, he shall not cease exerting himself in their behalf.

LEIGH HUNT TO J. F. (JOHN FORSTER?).

WIMBLEDON, August 11 and 12, 1846.

. . . I find I made a great confusion of my *portion* of the legal expenses incurred by the *Examiner* with the *whole* of them. That portion only amounted to 750*l.*, the whole being 1,500*l.* Of this 750*l.* out of my pocket (which was quite enough), 250*l.* went to pay for expenses (counsel, etc.) attendant on the *failure* of two government prosecutions,—one for saying (*totidem verbis*) that " of all monarchs since the Revolution, the successor of George the Third would have the finest opportunity of becoming nobly popular " ; (think, nowadays, of being prosecuted for *that !*) and the other for copying from the *Stamford News* the paragraph against military flogging, alluded to the other day in the *Daily News.* (Think, now, this moment, of being prosecuted for THAT !) The 500*l.* fine and two years' imprisonment was for ludicrously contrasting the *Morning Post's* picture of the Regent as an " Adonis," etc., with the old and real fat state of the case, and for adding that his Royal Highness had lived for " upwards of half a century without doing any thing to deserve the admiration of his contemporaries or the gratitude of posterity." Words to that effect, and I believe better,—but I do not quite remember them. They might be easily ascertained by reference to Peel's Coffee-house, and the words of the *Post* too.*

* In 1813 Hunt was sent to jail for satirizing the Prince Regent ; in 1845 Thackeray published, in *Punch*, an epitaph upon George IV., and there seems to have been no attempt made to punish him for his temerity. Thirty years had wrought great changes in England, and it was now safe to speak the truth, even about royalty. The epitaph (one of a series of brief sketches of the Georges) is not to be found in many editions of Thackeray's works, and may be new to some readers :

" Georgius Ultimus:
" He left an example for age and for youth
    To avoid.
He never acted well by Man or Woman,
And was as false to his Mistress as to his Wife.
He deserted his Friends and his Principles.
He was so Ignorant that he could scarcely Spell ;
    But he had some Skill in Cutting out Coats,
        And an undeniable Taste for Cookery.
He built the Palaces of Brighton and of Buckingham,
        And for these qualities and Proofs of Genius,
            An admiring Aristocracy
Christened him the ' First Gentleman in Europe.'
    Friends, respect the KING whose Statue is here,
And the generous Aristocracy who admired him."

Besides the fine, my imprisonment cost me several hundred pounds (I can't exactly say how many) in monstrous *douceurs* to the gaoler for *liberty to walk in the garden*, for help towards getting me permission to fit up rooms in the sick hospital, and for fitting up said rooms, or rather converting them from sorts of wash-houses, hitherto uninhabited and unfloored, into comfortable apartments,—which I did too expensively,—at least as far as papering the sitting-room with a trellis of roses went, and having my ceiling painted to imitate an out-of-door sky. . . .

THOMAS CARLYLE TO THOMAS MURRAY.

ANNAN, August, 1814.

O Tom, what a foolish flattering creature thou art! To talk of future eminence in connection with the literary history of the nineteenth century to such a one as me! Alas! my good lad, when I and all my fancies and reveries and speculations shall have been swept over with the besom of oblivion, the literary history of no century will feel itself the worse. Yet think not, because I talk thus, I am careless of literary fame. No; Heaven knows that ever since I have been able to form a wish, the wish of being known has been the foremost.

O Fortune! thou that givest unto each his portion in this dirty planet, bestow (if it shall please thee) coronets, and crowns, and principalities, and purses, and pudding, and powers upon the great and noble and fat ones of the earth. Grant me that, with a heart of independence unyielding to thy favors and unbending to thy frowns, I may attain to literary fame ; and though starvation be my lot, I will smile that I have not been born a king.

But alas! my dear Murray, what am I, or what are you, or what is any other poor unfriended stripling in the ranks of learning? . . .

THOMAS CARLYLE TO HIS MOTHER.

EDINBURGH, January 10, 1821.

. . . I am afraid that you take my case too deeply to heart. It is true, I am toiling on the waves, and my vessel looks but like a light canoe, yet surely the harbor is before me, and in soberness when I compare my tackle with that of others,' I cannot doubt hardly that I shall get within the pier at last. Without figure, I am not a genius, but a rather sharp youth, discontented and partly mismanaged, ready to work at aught but teaching, and to be satisfied with the ordinary recompense of every honest son of Adam, food and raiment and common respectability. Can I fail to get them if I continue steadfast? No, I cannot fail. The way, indeed, is weary; it leads through a dry, parched land wherein few waters be; but how happy it is that I journey unattended by Remorse! that my conscience, though it wound, does not sting me; that my heart, when it faints, does not condemn! I ought to be grateful that it is so; and to bear these " light afflictions " calmly—they are not sent without need.

You observe, Mother, I talk about my own affairs most fluently, yet there are other affairs about which I am any thing rather than indifferent. It will be changing the direction more than the nature of my thoughts (for this also is one of *my* concerns) if I inquire particularly into your situation at Mainhill. *How* are you? Tell me largely when you write. I hear your health is feeble; I conjure you to be careful of it. Do you get tea—the weary tea—*alone* now? By the little table *ben* the house? I advise you to use it frequently ; it is excellent for weak stomachs. And do not, I entreat you, let any considerations of thrift or such things restrain you in those cases. None of us is rich, but we should certainly be poor indeed if among us we could not muster enough for such a purpose. Keep yourself from cold most carefully this unhealthy season, and read the *Worthies* or any thing that will satisfy that high enthusiasm of your mind, which, however you may disbelieve it, is quite of a piece with my own. Do you still get the *Repository ?* I observe there is to be a fresh Magazine at Glasgow, embracing the interests of the *United* Secession Church. I wish it could be got for you.

But here I must end. A happy new year to you, my dear Mother, and many, many of them —to be a blessing to us all ! Write to me next time in the most ample manner. My best love to all the children.

———

THOMAS CARLYLE TO HIS BROTHER, JOHN CARLYLE.

EDINBURGH, March, 1822.

. . . My condition is rather strange at present. I feel as if I were impelled to write ; as if I had also very little power to do it ; but

at the same time as if I had altogether lost the
faculty of exerting that power. It is these
"coorsed nervous disorders." If I had but
strong health! But what is the use of talking? If I had a supereminent genius, the end
would be still better attained, and the wish is
perhaps just about as reasonable. Should I
never be healthy again, it will not aid me to
complain, to sit and whine, "put finger in the
eye and sob," because my longings are not
gratified. Better to do what I can while it is
called to-day; and if the edifice I create be but
a dog-hutch, it is more honorable to have built
a dog-hutch than to have dreamed of building
a palace. Therefore, Jack, I mean to try if I
can bestir myself. Art is long and life is short;
and of the threescore and ten years allotted to
the liver, how small a portion is spent in any
thing but vanity and vice, if not in wretched-
ness, and worse than unprofitable struggling with
the adamantine laws of fate! I am wae when
I think of all this, but it cannot be helped.

THOMAS CARLYLE TO RALPH WALDO EMERSON.

LONDON, February 8, 1839.

. . . This foggy Babylon tumbles along as it
was wont; and as for my particular case, uses

me, not worse, but better, than of old. Nay,
there are many in it that have a real friendliness
for me. For example, the other night a massive portmanteau of books, sent according to
my written list, from the Cambridge University
Library, from certain friends there whom I have
never seen: a gratifying arrival; for we have
no library here from which we can borrow
books home, and are only in these weeks striving to get one. Think of that! The worst is
the sore tear and wear of this huge roaring
Niagara of things on such a poor excitable set
of nerves as mine. The velocity of all things,
of the very word you hear on the streets, is at
railway rate. Joy itself is unenjoyable, to be
avoided like pain. There is no wish one has
so pressing as for quiet. Ah me! I often swear
I will be *buried* at least in free breezy Scotland,
out of this insane hubbub, where Fate tethers
me in life! If Fate always tether me;—but if
ever the smallest competence of worldly means
be mine, I will fly this whirlpool as I would the
lake of *Malebolge,* and only visit it now and
then! Yet perhaps it is the proper place after
all, seeing all places are *im*proper; who knows?
Meanwhile I lead a most dyspeptic, solitary,
self-shrouded life; consuming, if possible in si-

lence, my considerable allotment of pain, glad when any strength is left in me for working, which is the only use I can see in myself—too rare a case of late. The ground of my existence is black as Death ; too black, when all *void*, too ; but at times there paint themselves on it pictures of gold and rainbow and lightning; all the brighter for the background, I suppose. Withal I am very much of a fool. Some people will have me write on *Cromwell*, which I have been talking about. I do read on that and English subjects, finding that I know nothing, and that nobody knows any thing of that ; but whether any thing will come of it remains to be seen. . . .

THOMAS ARNOLD TO F. C. BLACKSTONE.

RUGBY, September 28, 1828.

It is, indeed, a long time since I wrote to you, and there has been much of intense interest in the period which has elapsed since I did write. But it has been quite an engrossing occupation; and Thucydides and every thing else has gone to sleep while I have been attending to it. Now it is becoming more familiar to me, but still the actual employment of time is very

great, and the matters for thought which it af-
fords are almost endless. Still I get my daily
exercise and bathing, very happily, so that I
have been, and am, perfectly well, and equal
in strength and spirits to the work. . . . For
myself, I like it hitherto beyond my expectation ; but of course a month is a very short
time to judge from. I am trying to establish
something of a friendly intercourse with the
Sixth Form, by asking them, in succession, in
parties of four, to dinner with us, and I have
them each separately up into my room to look
over their exercises. . . . I mean to bring in
something like " gatherings " before it is long,
for they understand that I have not done with
my alterations, nor probably ever shall have ;
and I am going to have an examination for
every form in the school, at the end of the short
half-year, in all the business of the half year,
Divinity, Greek and Latin, Arithmetic, History,
Geography, and Chronology, with first and second classes, and prize-books for those who do
well. I find that my power is perfectly absolute, so that I have no excuse if I do not try
to make the school something like my beau
ideal—it is sure to fall far enough short in real-

ity.   There has been no flogging yet (and I hope that there will be none), and surprisingly few irregularities.   I chastise, at first, by very gentle impositions, which are raised for a repetition of offences—flogging will be only my ratio ultima—and *talking* I shall try to the utmost. I believe that boys may be governed a great deal by gentle methods and kindness, and appealing to their better feelings, if you show that you are not afraid of them.   I have seen great boys, six feet high, shed tears when I have sent for them up into my room and spoken to them quietly, in private, for not knowing their lesson ; and I have found that this treatment produced its effects afterwards in making them do better. But of course, deeds must second words when needful, or words will soon be laughed at.

THOMAS ARNOLD TO JOHN TAYLOR COLERIDGE.

RUGBY, October 12, 1835.

. . . I cannot tell you, how I enjoyed our fortnight at Rugby before the school opened. It quite reminded me of Oxford, when Mary and I used to sit out in the garden under the enormous elms of the school-field, which almost overhang the house, and saw the line of our battlemented roofs and the pinnacles and cross of our chapel cutting the unclouded sky. And I had divers happy little matches at cricket with my own boys in the school-field, on the very cricket-ground of the " eleven," that is, of the best players in the school, on which, when the school is assembled, no profane person may encroach. . . . It would overpay me for far greater uneasiness and labor than I have ever had at Rugby, to see the feeling both towards the school and towards myself person-ally with which some of our boys have been lately leaving us. One stayed with us in the house for his last week at Rugby, dreading the approach of the day which should take him to Oxford, although he was going up to a most delightful society of old friends ; and, when he actually came to take his leave, I really think that the parting was like that of a father and his son. And it is delightful to me to find how glad all the better boys are to come back here after they have left it, and how much they seem to enjoy staying with me; while a sure instinct keeps at a distance all whose recollec-tions of the place are connected with uncom-fortable reflections. Meantime I write nothing, and read barely enough to keep my mind in the state of a running stream, which I think it ought to be if it would form and feed other minds; for it is ill drinking out of a pond, whose stock of water is merely the remains of the long past rains of the winter and spring, evaporating and diminishing with every successive day of drought. . . .

CHARLES KINGSLEY TO PETER A. L. H. WOOD.

EVERSLEY, 1842.

Peter!—Whether in the glaring saloons of Almack's, or making love in the equestrian stateliness of the park, or the luxurious recumbency of the ottoman, whether breakfasting at one, or going to bed at three, thou art still Peter, the beloved of my youth, the staff of my academic days, the regret of my parochial retirement!—Peter! I am alone! Around me are the everlasting hills, and the everlasting bores of the country! My parish is peculiar for nothing but want of houses and abundance of peat bogs; my parishioners remarkable only for aversion to education, and a predilection for fat bacon. I am wasting my sweetness on the desert air—I say my sweetness, for I have

given up smoking, and smell no more. O
Peter, Peter, come down and see me! O that
I could behold your head towering above the
fir-trees that surround my lonely dwelling.
Take pity on me! I am like a kitten in the
washhouse copper with the lid on! And, Peter,
prevail on some of your friends here to give
me a day's trout-fishing, for my hand is getting
out of practice. But, Peter, I am, considering
the oscillations and perplex circumgurgitations
of this piece-meal world, an improved man. I
am much more happy, much more comfortable,
reading, thinking, and doing my duty—much
more than ever I did before in my life. Therefore I am not discontented with my situation,
or regretful that I buried my first-class in a
country curacy, like the girl who shut herself
up in a band-box on her wedding night (*vide*
Rogers' "Italy"). And my lamentations are
not general (for I do not want an inundation of
the froth and tide-wash of Babylon the Great),
but particular, being solely excited by want of
thee, O Peter, who art very pleasant to me,
and wouldst be more so if thou wouldst come
and eat my mutton, and drink my wine, and
admire my sermons, some Sunday at Eversley.

Vol. I.

CHARLES KINGSLEY TO JOHN BULLAR.

EVERSLEY, January 27, 1857.

. . . I feel deeply the change in one's imagination during the last twenty years. As a child I never could distinguish dreams from imaginations, imaginations from waking impressions, and was often thought to be romancing when I was relating a real impression. In ill-health from overwork about sixteen to eighteen, I had spectral illusions often (one as clear as any of Nicolai's), accompanied with frightful nervous excitability, and inability to settle to any work, though always working at something in a fierce, desultory way. At twenty I found out tobacco. The spectres vanished ; the power of dull application arose, and for the first time in my life I began to be master of my own brain.

Now I am in general the most prosaic and matter-of-fact of parsons. I cannot dream if I try. I go to my brain as to a store-house or carpenter's shop, from which I take out coolly what I want, and put it into the best shape I can. The German mode of thought, feeling, and writing, such as you find in Jean Paul or Novalis, lies behind me, as " boy's love " belonging to an era " when the spirits of the prophets "

were not yet "subject to the prophets."
Whether this be right or wrong, I know not;
but I confess the fact;—and if we ever get a
week together, I fear that you will think me a
most dull and frivolous fellow, who cares for
nothing but to romp with your children, and
pick flowers, and study the weather *usque ad
nauseam.*

But here lies the difference between us.
Your work is utterly of the head; and you go
for amusement to fancy, to imagination, to
metaphysic. My work, whether parish or writing, lies just in the sphere wherein you play,
and if I played in that sphere, too, I should go
mad, or soften my brain, like poor Southey.
So when I play, I think about nothing; ride,
fish, chat with the farmers over the crops, examine beetles and worms, and forget that I
have a heart as much as I can. But I won't
bore you more about myself.

SYDNEY SMITH TO LADY HOLLAND.

HESLINGTON, September 9, 1809.

I hear you laugh at me for being happy in
the country, and upon this I have a few words
to say. In the first place, whether one lives or

dies, I hold, and have always held, to be of infinitely less moment than is generally supposed; but if life is to be, then it is common-sense to amuse yourself with the best you can find where you happen to be placed. I am not leading precisely the life I should choose, but that which (all things considered, as well as I could consider them) appeared to me to be the most eligible. I am resolved, therefore, to like it, and to reconcile myself to it; which is more manly than to feign myself above it, and to send up complaints by the post, of being thrown away, and being desolate, and such like trash. I am prepared, therefore, either way. If the chances of life ever enable me to emerge, I will show you that I have not been wholly occupied by small and sordid pursuits. If (as the greater probability is) I am come to the end of my career, I give myself quietly up to horticulture, etc. In short, if it be my lot to crawl, I will crawl contentedly; if to fly, I will fly with alacrity; but, as long as I can possibly avoid it, I will never be unhappy. If, with a a pleasant wife, three children, a good house and farm, many books, and many friends, who wish me well, I cannot be happy, I am a very silly, foolish fellow, and what becomes of me is of very little consequence. I have at least this chance of doing well in Yorkshire, that I am heartily tired of London.

I beg pardon for saying so much of myself, but I say it upon this subject once for all. . . .

SYDNEY SMITH TO M. EUGÈNE ROBIN.

LONDON, June 29, 1844.

. . . I am seventy-four years of age ; and being Canon of St. Paul's in London, and a rector of a parish in the country, my time is divided equally between town and country. I am living among the best society in the metropolis, and at ease in my circumstances ; in tolerable health, a mild Whig, a tolerating Churchman, and much given to talking, laughing, and noise. I dine with the rich in London, and physic the poor in the country ; passing from the sauces of Dives to the sores of Lazarus. I am, upon the whole, a happy man ; have found the world an entertaining world, and am thankful to Providence for the part allotted to me in it. If you wish to become more informed respecting the actor himself, I must refer you to my friend Van de Weyer, who knows me well, and

is able (if he will condescend to do so) to point
out the good and the evil within me. If you
come to London, I hope you will call on me,
and enable me to make your acquaintance;
and in the meantime I beg you to accept every
assurance of my consideration and respect.

———

SYDNEY SMITH TO LORD JOHN RUSSELL.

April 3, 1837.

. . . I defy —— to quote a single passage
of my writing contrary to the doctrines of the
Church of England ; for I have always avoided
speculative, and preached practical, religion. I
defy him to mention a single action in my life
which he can call immoral. The only thing he
could charge me with would be high spirits, and
much innocent nonsense. I am distinguished
as a preacher, and sedulous as a parochial cler-
gyman. His real charge is, that I am a high-
spirited, honest, uncompromising man, whom
all the bench of bishops could not turn, and
who would set them all at defiance upon great
and vital questions. This is the reason why
(as far as depends upon others) I am not a
bishop ; but I am thoroughly sincere in saying
I would not take any bishopric whatever, and

to this I pledge my honor and character as a
gentleman. But, had I been a bishop, you
would have seen me, on a late occasion, char-
ging —— and —— with a gallantry which would
have warmed your heart's blood, and made
Melbourne rub the skin off his hands. . . .

SYDNEY SMITH TO LADY HOLLAND.

December 28, 1839.

I will dine with you on Saturday, my dear
Lady Holland, with the greatest pleasure.

I have written against —— one of the clev-
erest pamphlets I ever read, which I think
would cover —— and him with ridicule. At
least it made me laugh very much in reading
it ; and there I stood, with the printer's devil,
and the real Devil close to me ; and then I
said : " After all, this is very funny, and very
well written, but it will give great pain to people who have been very kind and good to me
through life ; and what can I do to show my
sense of that kindness, if it is not by flinging
this pamphlet into the fire ? " So I flung it in,
and there was an end ! My sense of ill usage
remains, of course, the same. . . .

THOMAS BABINGTON MACAULAY TO THOMAS
FLOWER ELLIS.

CALCUTTA, December 30, 1835.

. . . What my course of life will be, when
I return to England, is very doubtful. But I
am more than half determined to abandon politics, and to give myself wholly to letters ; to
undertake some great historical work which
may be at once the business and the amusement of my life ; and to leave the pleasures
of pestiferous rooms, sleepless nights, aching
heads, and diseased stomachs to Roebuck and
to Praed.

In England I might probably be of a very
different opinion. But, in the quiet of my own
little grass-plot,—when the moon, at its rising,
finds me with the Philoctetes or the De Finibus
in my hand,—I often wonder what strange in-
fatuation leads men who can do something
better to squander their intellect, their health,
their energy, on such objects as those which
most statesmen are engaged in pursuing. I
comprehend perfectly how a man who can debate, but who would make a very indifferent
figure as a contributor to an annual or a magazine,—such a man as Stanley, for example,—

should take the only line by which he can
attain distinction. But that a man before
whom the two paths of literature and politics
lie open, and who might hope for eminence in
either, should choose politics, and quit literature, seems to me madness. On the one side
is health, leisure, peace of mind, the search after
truth, and all the enjoyments of friendship and
conversation. On the other side is almost certain ruin to the constitution, constant labor,
constant anxiety. Every friendship which a
man may have becomes precarious as soon as
he engages in politics. As to abuse, men soon
become callous to it ; but the discipline which
makes them callous is very severe. And for
what is it that a man who might, if he chose,
rise and lie down at his own hour, engage in
any study, enjoy any amusements, and visit
any place, consents to make himself as much a
prisoner as if he were within the rules of the
Fleet ; to be tethered during eleven months of
the year within the circle of half a mile round
Charing Cross ; to sit, or stand, night after
night for ten or twelve hours, inhaling a noi-
some atmosphere, and listening to harangues
of which nine tenths are far below the level of

a leading article in a newspaper? For what is it that he submits, day after day, to see the morning break over the Thames, and then totters home, with bursting temples, to his bed? Is it for fame? Who would compare the fame of Charles Townshend to that of Hume, that of Lord North to that of Gibbon ; that of Lord Chatham to that of Johnson? Who can look back on the life of Burke, and not regret that the years which he passed in ruining his health and temper by political exertions were not passed in the composition of some great and durable work? Who can read the letters to Atticus, and not feel that Cicero would have been an infinitely happier and better man, and a not less celebrated man, if he had left us fewer speeches and more Academic Questions and Tusculan Disputations ; if he had passed the time which he spent in brawling with Vatinius and Clodius in producing a history of Rome superior even to that of Livy? But these, as I said, are meditations in a quiet garden, situated far beyond the contagious influence of English faction. What I might feel if I again saw Downing Street and Palace Yard is another question. I tell you sincerely my present feelings. . . .

SIR WALTER SCOTT TO GEORGE CRABBE.

ASHESTIEL, October 21, 1809.

I am just honored with your letter, which gives me the more sensible pleasure, since it has gratified a wish of more than twenty years' standing. It is, I think, fully that time since I was, for great part of a very snowy winter, the inhabitant of an old house in the country, in a course of poetical study, so very like that of your admirably painted " Young Lad," that I could hardly help saying, " That 's me ! " when I was reading the tale to my family. Among the very few books which fell under my hands was a volume or two of Dodsley's Annual Register, one of which contained copious extracts from " The Village " and " The Library," particularly the conclusion of book first of the former, and an extract from the latter, beginning with the description of the old romancers. I committed them most faithfully to my memory, where your verses must have felt themselves very strangely lodged in company with ghost stories, border riding-ballads, scraps of old plays, and all the miscellaneous stuff which a strong appetite for reading, with neither means nor discrimination for selection, had assembled in the head of a lad of eighteen. New

publications, at that time, were very rare in Edinburgh, and my means of procuring them very
limited ; so that, after a long search for the poems which contained these beautiful specimens,
and which had afforded me so much delight, I
was fain to rest contented with the extracts
from the Register, which I could repeat at this
moment. You may, therefore, guess my sincere delight when I saw your poems at a later
period assume the rank in the public consideration which they so well deserve. It was a triumph to my own immature taste to find I had
anticipated the applause of the learned and of
the critical, and I became very desirous to offer
my *gratulor*, among the more important plaud-
its which you have had from every quarter. . . .
I am too proud of the compliments you honor
me with, to affect to decline them ; and with
respect to the comparative view I have of my
own labors and yours, I can only assure you
that none of my little folks, about the formation of whose taste and principles I may be
supposed naturally solicitous, have ever read
any of my own poems ; while yours have been
our regular evening's amusement. My eldest
girl begins to read well, and enters as well into

the humor as into the sentiment of your admirable descriptions of human life. As for rivalry, I think it has seldom existed among those who know, by experience, that there are much better things in the world than literary reputation, and that one of the best of these good things is the regard and friendship of those deservedly and generally esteemed for their worth or their talents. I believe many dilettanti authors do cocker themselves up into a great jealousy of anything that interferes with what they are pleased to call their fame ; but I should as soon think of nursing one of my own fingers into a whitlow for my private amusement, as encouraging such a feeling. . . .

SIR WALTER SCOTT TO J. B. S. MORRITT.

EDINBURGH, July 9, 1814.

. . . Now, to go from one important subject to another, I must account for my own laziness, which I do by referring you to a small anonymous sort of a novel, in three volumes—Waverley—which you will receive by the mail of this day. It was a very old attempt of mine to embody some traits of those characters and manners peculiar to Scotland, the last remnants

of which vanished during my own youth, so
that few or no traces now remain. I had written great part of the first volume, and sketched
other passages, when I mislaid the MS., and
only found it by the merest accident as I was
rummaging the drawers of an old cabinet ; and
I took the fancy of finishing it, which I did so
fast, that the last two volumes were written in
three weeks. I had a great deal of fun in the
accomplishment of this task, though I do not
expect that it will be popular in the south, as
much of the humor, if there be any, is local,
and some of it even professional. You, however, who are an adopted Scotchman, will find
some amusement in it. It has made a very
strong impression here, and the good people of
Edinburgh are busied in tracing the author, and
in finding out originals for the portraits it contains. In the first case, they will probably find
it difficult to convict the guilty author, although
he is far from escaping suspicion. Jeffrey has
offered to make oath that it is mine, and another great critic has tendered his affidavit, *ex
contrario ;* so that these authorities have divided the gude town. However, the thing has
succeeded very well, and is thought highly of.
I don't know if it has got to London yet. I in-

tend to maintain my *incognito.* Let me know
your opinion about it. . . .

WILLIAM MAKEPEACE THACKERAY TO ABRAHAM
HAYWARD.

KENSINGTON, February 1, 1850.

Thank you for your kind note. I was quite
prepared for the issue of the kind effort made
at the Athenæum in my behalf. Indeed, as a
satirical writer, I rather wonder that I have not
made more enemies than I have. I don't mean
enemies in a bad sense, but men conscientiously
opposed to my style, art, opinions, imperti-
nences, and so forth. There must be thou-
sands of men to whom the practice of ridicule
must be offensive ; does n't one see such in
society, or in one's own family,—Persons whose
nature was not gifted with a sense of humor?
Such a man would be wrong not to give me a
blackball, or whatever it is called—a negatory
nod of his honest, respectable, stupid old head.
And I submit to his verdict without the slightest feeling of animosity against my judge.
Why, Doctor Johnson would certainly have
blackballed Fielding, whom he pronounced "A
dull fellow, sir, a dull fellow !" And why
should n't my friend at the Athenæum? About

getting in I don't care twopence; but indeed I
am very much pleased to have had such sureties
as Hallam and Milman, and to know that the
gentlemen whom you mention were so generous
in their efforts to serve me. What does the
rest matter? If you should ever know the old
gentleman (for old I am sure he is, steady and
respectable) who objects to me, give him my
best compliments, and say I think he was quite
right to exercise his judgment honestly, and to
act according to that reason with which Heaven
has mercifully endowed him. But that he
would be slow, I would n't in the least object
to meet him; and he in his turn would think
me flippant, etc. Enough of these egotisms.
Did n't I tell you once before that I feel frightened almost at the kindness of people regard-
ing me? May we all be honest fellows, and
keep our heads from too much vanity. . . .

WILLIAM MAKEPEACE THACKERAY TO WILLIAM
B. REED.

WASHINGTON, 1853.

. . . There are half a dozen houses I already
know in Philadelphia * where I could find very

* Mr. Reed had urged Mr. Thackeray to obtain the British
Consulate in Philadelphia.

pleasant friends and company; and that good old library would give me plenty of acquaintances more. But, home among my parents there, and some few friends I have made in the last twenty-five years, and a tolerably fair prospect of an honest livelihood on the familiar London flagstones, and the library at the Athenæum, and the ride in the park, and the pleasant society afterwards, and a trip to Paris now and again, and to Switzerland and Italy in the summer—these are little temptations which make me not discontented with my lot, about which I grumble only for pastime, and because it is an Englishman's privilege. Own, now, that all these recreations here enumerated have a pleasant sound. I hope I shall live to enjoy them yet a little while before I go to "*nox et domus exilis Plutonia.*" . . .

I never feel pity for a man dying; only for survivors, if there be such passionately deploring him. You see the pleasures the undersigned proposes to himself here in future years—a sight of the Alps, a holiday on the Rhine, a ride in the park, a colloquy with pleasant friends of an evening. If it is death to part with these delights (and pleasures they are, and no mistake), sure the mind can conceive others afterwards; and I know one small philosopher who is quite ready to give up these pleasures; quite content (after a pang or two of separation from dear friends here) to put his hand into that of the summoning angel, and say, " Lead on, O messenger of God our Father, to the next place whither the divine goodness calls us!" We must be blindfolded before we can pass, I know; but I have no fear about what is to come, any more than my children need fear that the love of *their* father should fail them. I thought myself a dead man once, and protest the notion gave me no disquiet about myself—at least the philosophy is more comfortable than that which is tinctured with brimstone. . . .

WILLIAM MAKEPEACE THACKERAY TO WILLIAM B. REED.

NEUCHATEL, July 21, 1853.

. . . Three weeks of London were more than enough for me, and I feel as if I had had enough of it and pleasure. Then I remained a month with my parents; then I brought my girls on a little pleasuring tour. We spent ten days at Baden, when I set intrepidly to work again, and have been five days in Switzerland now; not

bent on going up mountains, but on taking
things easily. How beautiful it is! How pleasant! How great and affable, too, the landscape
is! It 's delightful to be in the midst of such
scenes; the ideas get generous reflections from
them. I don't mean to say my thoughts grow
mountainous and enormous like the Alpine
chain yonder; but in fine, it is good to be in
the presence of this noble nature; it is keeping
good company; keeping away mean thoughts.
I see in the papers, now and again, accounts of
fine parties in London. *Bon dieu!* Is it possible any one ever wanted to go to fine London
parties; and are there now people sweating in
Mayfair routs? The European continent
swarms with your people. They are not all as
polished as Chesterfield. I wish some of them
spoke French a little better. I saw five of them
at supper at Basle the other night with their
knives down their throats. It was awful. My
daughter saw it; and I was obliged to say : "My
dear, your great-great-grandmother, one of the
finest ladies of the old school I ever saw, always
applied cold steel to her wittles. It 's no *crime*
to eat with a knife "; which is all very well;
but I wish five of 'em at a time would n't. . . .

GLIMPSES OF MEN AND WOMEN.

WILLIAM GODWIN TO SAMUEL TAYLOR COLERIDGE.

DUBLIN, September, 1800.

You scarcely expected a letter from me of the above date. But I received last September an invitation from John Philpot Curran, the Irish barrister, probably the first advocate in Europe, then in London, to spend a few weeks with him in Ireland this summer, which I did not feel in myself philosophy enough to resist. Nor do I repent my compliance. The advantages one derives from placing the sole of one's foot on a foreign soil are extremely great. Few men, on such an occasion, think it worth their while to put on armor for your encounter. I know Fox and Sheridan, but can scarce consider them as my acquaintance. Your next-door neighbor, before he admits you to his familiarity, considers how far he should like to have you for his familiar for the next seven years. But familiarity with a foreign guest involves no such consequences, and so circumstanced, you are immediately admitted on the footing of an inmate. I am now better acquainted with Grattan and Curran, the Fox and Sheridan of Ireland, after having been four weeks in their company, than I can pretend ever to have been with their counterparts on my native soil.

Curran I admire extremely. There is scarcely the man on earth with whom I ever felt myself so entirely at my ease, or so little driven back, from time to time, to consider of my own miserable individual. He is perpetually a staff and a cordial, without ever affecting to be either. The being never lived who was more perfectly free from every species of concealment. With great genius, at least a rich and inexhaustible imagination, he never makes me stand in awe of him, and bow as to my acknowledged superior, a thing by-the-by which, *de temps à d'autre,* you compel me to do. He amuses me always, astonishes me often, yet naturally and irresistibly inspires me with confidence. I am apt, particularly when away from home, to feel forlorn and dispirited. The two last days I spent from him, and though they were employed most enviably in *tête à tête* with Grattan, I began to feel dejected and home-sick. But Curran has joined me to-day, and poured into my bosom a full portion of his irresistible kindness and gaiety.

You will acknowledge these are extraordinary traits. Yet Curran is far from a faultless and perfect character. Immersed for many years in a perpetual whirl of business, he has no profoundness or philosophy. He has a great share of the Irish character—dashing, *étourdi*, coarse, vulgar, impatient, fierce, kittenish. He has no characteristic delicacy, no intuitive and instant commerce with the sublime features of nature. Ardent in a memorable degree, and a patriot from the most generous impulse, he has none of that political chemistry which Burke so admirably describes (I forget his words), that resolves and combines, and embraces distant nations and future ages. He is inconsistent in the most whimsical degree. I remember, in an amicable debate with Sheridan, in which Sheridan far outwent him in refinement, penetration, and taste, he three times surrendered his arms, acknowledged his error, yea, even began to declaim (for declamation is too frequently his mania) on the contrary side: and as often, after a short interval, resumed his weapons, and renewed the combat. Now and then, in the career of declamation, he becomes tautological and ineffective, and I ask myself: Is this the prophet that we went forth to see! But presently after he stumbles upon a rich vein of imagination, and recognizes my willing suffrage. He has the reputation of insincerity, for which he is indebted, not to his heart, but to the mistaken, cherished calculations of his practical prudence. He maintains in argument that you ought never to inform a man, directly or indirectly, of the high esteem in which you hold him. Yet, in his actual intercourse, he is apt to mix the information too copiously and too often. But perhaps his greatest fault is, that though endowed with an energy the most ardent, and an imagination the most varied and picturesque, there is nothing to which he is more prone, or to which his inclination more willingly leads him, than to play the buffoon.

THOMAS CARLYLE TO RALPH WALDO EMERSON.

LONDON, June 24, 1839.

. . . Not many days ago I saw at breakfast the notablest of all your Notabilities,

Daniel Webster. He is a magnificent specimen ; you might say to all the world : This is
your Yankee Englishman, such Limbs *we* make
in Yankeeland ! As a Logic-fencer, Advocate,
or Parliamentary Hercules, one would incline
to back him at first sight against the extant
world. The tanned complexion, that amor-
phous crag-like face ; the dull black eyes under
the precipice of brows, like dull anthracite fur-
naces, needing only to be *blown ;* the mastiff-
mouth, accurately closed :—I have not traced
as much of *silent Berserkir-rage*, that I remember of, in any other man. " I guess I should
not like to be your nigger ! "—Webster is not
loquacious, but he is pertinent, conclusive ; a
dignified, perfectly bred man, though not English in breeding : a man worthy of the best
reception from us ; and meeting such, I understand. He did not speak much with me that
morning, but seemed not at all to dislike
me. . . .

MISS MARY RUSSELL MITFORD TO MISS EMILY
JEPHSON.

THREE-MILE CROSS, September 21, 1839.

. . . Daniel Webster is himself not more
than fifty-five now—the first lawyer, orator,

and statesman of America, certainly, and the next, or next but one, President. He is the noblest-looking man I ever saw, both in face and person. The portrait prefixed to his " Speeches " does him great injustice, for his countenance is delightfully gracious—such a smile! and he is a broad, muscular, splendid figure. His manner, too, is all that one can imagine of calm, and sweet, and gracious—as charming as the Duke of Devonshire ; as courteous even as that prince of courtesy, and equally free from condescension—whilst amidst the perfect simplicity and gentleness there is great conversational power. His wife and daughters seem to adore his very footsteps ; and he has conquered for himself a degree of real consideration and respect in London never shown before to any transatlantic personage ; least of all to a lion. My father adores him. I think he liked him even better than I did ; and he says that he promised him to come again, and that he is sure he will keep his word.

I should like you to see Daniel Webster ! When I tell you that expecting from him what I did, and hearing from twenty people, accustomed to see in perfect intimacy all distinguished

people, that he alone gave them the idea of a
truly great man—when I say that he exceeded
our expectations by very far, you may imagine
what he is. I am to send them all my flower-
seeds, and they are to send me all theirs. I
chose the Murder Speech (is it not wonderfully
fine? like Sheil, without the tawdriness, I
think) to read to my father, because *that* is
free from the alloy, to an English ear, of allu-
sions intelligible across the water, but not to
us. Two very clever friends of ours went to
Oxford to hear him speak, and they say that
they would walk there again and back, to hear
him only speak the same speech over again!
Is not that praise? . . .

THOMAS BABINGTON MACAULAY TO MISS HANNAH
MORE MACAULAY.

LONDON, July 11, 1831.

Since I wrote to you I have been out to dine
and sleep at Holland House. . . .

In the evening Lord John Russell came:
and, soon after, old Talleyrand. I had seen
Talleyrand in very large parties, but had never
been near enough to hear a word that he said.
I now had the pleasure of listening for an hour

and a half to his conversation. He is certainly
the greatest curiosity that I ever fell in with.
His head is sunk down between two high shoulders. One of his feet is hideously distorted.
His face is as pale as that of a corpse, and
wrinkled to a frightful degree. His eyes have
an odd glassy stare quite peculiar to them. His
hair, thickly powdered and pomatumed, hangs
down his shoulders on each side as straight as
a pound of tallow-candles. His conversation,
however, soon makes you forget his ugliness
and infirmities. There is a poignancy without
effort in all that he says, which reminded me a
little of the character which the wits of Johnson's circle give of Beauclerk. . . .

———

FRANCIS JEFFREY TO HENRY COCKBURN.

LONDON, February 5, 1832.

. . . Talleyrand is more natural, plain, and
reasonable than I had expected ; a great deal
of the repose of high breeding and old age,
with a mild and benevolent manner, and great
calmness of speech, rather than the sharp,
caustic, cutting speech of a practised utterer of
bons mots. He spoke a great deal of old times
and old persons, the court of Louis XVI., when

Dauphin, his coronation, Voltaire, Malherbe, Turgot ; with traditional anecdotes of Massillon and Bossuet, and many women of those days, whose names I have forgotten, and a good deal of diplomatic anecdote, altogether very pleasing and easy. He did not eat much, nor talk much about eating, except only that he inquired very earnestly into the nature of *cocky-leekie*, and wished much to know whether *prunes* were essential. He settled at last that they should be boiled in the soup, but not brought up in it. He drank little but iced water. . . .

ROBERT SOUTHEY TO C. W. W. WYNN.

KESWICK, November 4, 1818,

. . . Wilberforce has been here with all his household, and such a household ! The principle of the family seems to be that, provided the servants have faith, good works are not to be expected from them, and the utter disorder which prevails in consequence is truly farcical. The old coachman would figure upon the stage. Upon making some complaint about the horses, he told his master and mistress that since they had been in this country they had been so lake-and-river-and-mountain-and-valley-mad, that they had thought of nothing that they ought to think of. I have seen nothing in such pell-mell, topsy-turvy, and chaotic confusion as Wilberforce's apartments since I used to see a certain breakfast-table in Skeleton Corner. His wife sits in the midst of it like Patience on a monument, and he frisks about as if every vein in his body were filled with quicksilver; but, withal, there is such a constant hilarity in every look and motion, such a sweetness in all his tones, such a benignity in all his thoughts, words, and actions, that all sense of his grotesque appearance is presently overcome, and you can feel nothing but love and admiration for a creature of so happy and blessed a nature.

MISS MARIA EDGEWORTH TO ———.

October, 1821.

. . . We have had Mr. Wilberforce for several days; and I cannot tell you how glad I am to have had an opportunity of hearing his delightful conversation, and of seeing the extent and variety of his abilities. He is not at all anxious to show himself off : he converses, he does not merely talk. His thoughts flow in such abundance, and from so many sources, that they often cross one another; and sometimes a reporter would be at a loss. As he literally seems to speak all his thoughts as they occur, he produces what strikes him on both sides of any question. This often puzzles his hearers, but to me it is a proof of candor and sincerity ; and it it is both amusing and instructive to see him thus balancing accounts aloud. He is very lively and full of odd contortions : no matter. His indulgent, benevolent temper strikes me particularly : he makes no pretension to superior sanctity or strictness. . . .

THOMAS CARLYLE TO JOHN A. CARLYLE.

KINNAIRD HOUSE, October 20, 1823.

. . . I stayed from Monday night till Thursday morning last with Johnstone. I had gone thither to meet Edward Irving and his spouse, though I did not effect this object till I returned to Dunkeld. . . . He himself is the same man as ever, only his mind seems churned into a foam by the late agitations, and is yielding a plentiful scum of vanities and harmless affectations. The hair of his head is like Nebuchadnezzar's when taken in from grass : he puckers up his face into various seamy peaks, rolls his eyes, and puffs like a blast furnace ; talking abundantly a flood of things, the body of which

is nonsense, but intermingled with sparkles of
curious thinking, and tinctured with his usual
flow of warm-hearted generosity and honest affection. We talked and debated, and the time
went pleasantly along. He was for me up to
London with him, for three months in summer,
to see the world, and so I might begin writing
in good earnest. I said nay—the offer being in-
compatible at present with my other engage-
ments, and at any rate savoring too much of
patronage to suit my taste. He is a kind, good
man, with many queer qualities, but with ab-
surdities of almost equal magnitude. He med-
itates things in which he must evidently fail; but
being what he is, he must always retain a high
place in the estimation of a certain portion of
the public. He and his beloved are returning
to Annan in a week or two, where they purpose
to make some stay. I shall always wish him
well, as men go, I know of no one like him. . . .

CHARLES LAMB TO LEIGH HUNT.

1825 (?).

. . . I have got acquainted with Mr. Irving,
the Scotch preacher, whose fame must have
reached you. He is an humble disciple at the
foot of Gamaliel S. T. C. Judge how his own

sectarists must stare, when I tell you he has
dedicated a book to S. T. C., acknowledging to
have learnt more of the nature of faith, Christianity, and Christian Church from him than
from all the men he ever conversed with! He
is a most amiable, sincere, modest man in a
room, this Boanerges in the temple.   Mrs.
Montagu told him the dedication would do him
no good. "That shall be a reason for doing
it," was his answer. Judge now, whether this
man be a quack. . . .

ROBERT SOUTHEY TO HIS WIFE.

LONDON, December 30, 1833.

We have been this morning to hear Rowland
Hill. . . .

Rowland, a fine, tall old man, with strong
features, very like his portrait, began by reading three verses for his text, stooping to the
book in a very peculiar manner.   Having done
this, he stood up erect and said: "Why, the
text is a sermon, and a very weighty one too."
I could not always follow his delivery, the loss
of his teeth rendering his words sometimes
indistinct, and the more so because his pronunciation is peculiar, generally giving *e* the sound

of *ai*, like the French. His manner was animated and striking, sometimes impressive and
dignified, always remarkable ; and so powerful
a voice I have rarely or never heard. Sometimes he took off his spectacles, frequently
stooped down to read a text, and on these
occasions he seemed to double his body, so
high did he stand. He told one or two familiar
stories, and used some odd expressions, such
as " A murrain on those who preach that when
we are sanctified we do not grow in grace ! "
and again : " I had almost said I had rather see
the Devil in the pulpit than an Antinomian ! "
The purport of his sermon was good ; nothing
fanatical, nothing enthusiastic ; and the Calvin-
ism which it expressed was so qualified as to be
harmless. The manner that of a performer, as
great in his line as Kean or Kemble, and the
manner it is which has attracted so large a con-
gregation about him, all of the better order of
persons in business. . . .

THOMAS BABINGTON MACAULAY TO HIS FATHER.

BRADFORD, July 26, 1826.

On Saturday I went to Sydney Smith's. His
parish lies three or four miles out of any fre-
quented road. He is, however, most pleasantly

situated. " Fifteen years ago," said he to me, as I alighted at the gate of his shrubbery, " I was taken up in Piccadilly and set down here. There was no house and no garden ; nothing but a bare field."

One service this eccentric divine has certainly rendered to the Church. He has built the very neatest, most commodious, and most appropriate rectory that I ever saw. All its decorations are in a peculiarly clerical style, grave, simple, and Gothic. The bed-chambers are excellent, and excellently fitted up ; the sitting-rooms handsome ; and the grounds sufficiently pretty. Tindal and Parke (not the judge, of course), two of the best lawyers, best scholars, and best men in England, were there. We passed an extremely pleasant evening, and had a very good dinner, and many amusing anecdotes. After breakfast the next morning I walked to church with Sydney Smith. The edifice is not at all in keeping with the rectory. It is a miserable little hovel with a wooden belfry. It was, however, well filled, and with decent people, who seemed to take very much to their pastor. I understand that he is a very respectable apothecary ; and most liberal of his skill, his medi-

cine, his soup, and his wine, among the sick.
He preached a very queer sermon—the former
half too familiar and the latter half too florid,
but not without some ingenuity of thought and
expression.

Sydney Smith brought me to York on Monday morning in time for the stage-coach which
runs to Skipton. We parted with many assur-
ances of good-will. I have really taken a great
liking to him. He is full of wit, humor, and
shrewdness. He is not one of those show
talkers who reserve all their good things for
special occasions. It seems to be his greatest
luxury to keep his wife and daughter laughing
two or three hours every day. His notions of
law, government, and trade are surprisingly
clear and just. His misfortune is to have
chosen a profession at once above him and below him. Zeal would have made him a prodigy;
formality and bigotry would have made him a
bishop; but he could neither rise to the duties
of his order, nor stoop to its degradations.

———

MISS HANNAH MORE TO ——

ADELPHI, 1776.

I imagine my last was not so ambiguous but
that you saw well enough I stayed in town to see

Hamlet, and I will venture to say that it was such an entertainment as will probably never again be exhibited to an admiring world. . . .

In every part he* filled the whole soul of the spectator, and transcended the most finished idea of the poet. The requisites for Hamlet are not only various but opposed. In him they are all united, and, as it were, concentrated. One thing I must particularly remark, that, whether in the stimulation of madness, in the sinkings of despair, in the familiarity of friendship, in the whirlwind of passion, or in the meltings of tenderness, he never once forgot he was a prince ; and in every variety of situation and transition of feeling, you discovered the highest polish of fine breeding and courtly manners.

Hamlet experiences the conflict of many passions and affections, but filial love ever takes the lead ; *that* is the great point from which he sets out, and to which he returns ; the others are all contingent and subordinate to it, and are cherished or renounced, as they promote or obstruct the operation of this leading principle. Had you seen with what exquisite art and skill

* Garrick.

Garrick maintained the subserviency of the less to the greater interests, you would agree with me, of what importance to the perfection of acting is that consummate good-sense which always pervades every part of his performances.

To the most eloquent expression of the eye, to the hand-writing of the passions on his features, to a sensibility which tears to pieces the hearts of his auditors, to powers so unparalleled, he adds a judgment of the most exquisite accuracy, the fruit of long experience and close observation, by which he preserves every gradation and transition of the passions, keeping all under the control of a just dependence and natural consistency. So naturally, indeed, do the ideas of the poet seem to mix with his own, that he seemed himself to be engaged in a succession of affecting situations, not giving utterance to a speech, but to the instantaneous expression of his feelings, delivered in the most affecting tones of voice, and with gestures that belong only to nature. It was a fiction as delightful as fancy, and as touching as truth. A few nights before, I saw him in "Abel Drugger"; and had I not seen him in both, I should

have thought it as possible for Milton to have
written "Hudibras," and Butler "Paradise
Lost," as for one man to have played "Hamlet" and "Drugger" with such excellence. I
found myself, not only in the best place, but
with the best company, in the house, for I sat
next the orchestra, in which were a number of
my acquaintance (and those no vulgar names),
Edmund and Richard Burke, Dr. Warton, and
Sheridan. . . .

JAMES BEATTIE TO MISS MARGARET VALENTINE.

EDINBURGH, May 28, 1784.

. . . The election of Scotch Peers; the meeting of Parliament; the state of parties; the old
and new ministry; Pitt and Fox; the General Assembly; all these things are now forgotten; and
nothing here is spoke of or thought of but Mrs.
Siddons. I have seen this wonderful person,
not only on the stage, but in private company;
for I passed two days with her at the Earl of
Buchan's. Her powers in tragedy are beyond
comparison great. I thought my old friend
Garrick fell little or nothing short of theatrical
perfection; and I have seen him in his prime,
and in his highest characters; but Garrick never
affected me half so much as Mrs. Siddons has

done. Indeed the heart that she cannot subdue must be made of other materials than flesh and blood. . . . In private company, Mrs. Siddons is a modest, unassuming, sensible women; of the gentlest and most elegant manners. Her moral character is not only unblemished, but exemplary. She is above the middle size, and I suppose about thirty-four years of age. Her countenance is the most interesting that can be; and, excepting the Duchess of Gordon, the most beautiful I have ever seen. Her eyes and eyebrows are of the deepest black. She loves music, and is fond of the Scotch tunes, many of which I played to her on the violoncello. One of them ("She rose and let me in," which you know is a favorite of mine) made the tears start from her eyes. "Go on," said she to me, "and you will soon have your revenge"; meaning that I would draw as many tears from her as she had drawn from me. She sung "Queen Mary's Complaint" to admiration : and I had the honor to accompany her on the bass. . . .

MISS MARIA EDGEWORTH TO ——
LONDON, February (?), 1822.

. . . Through Lydia White we have become more acquainted with Mrs. Siddons than I ever expected to be. She gave us the history of her first acting of Lady Macbeth, and of her resolving in the sleep-scene to lay down the candlestick, contrary to the precedent of Mrs. Pritchard and all the traditions, before she began to wash her hands and say, "Out, vile spot!" (*sic*).

Sheridan knocked violently at her door during the five minutes she had desired to have entirely to herself, to compose her spirits before the play began. He burst in, and prophesied that she would ruin herself forever if she persevered in this resolution *to lay down the candlestick*. She persisted, however, in her determination, succeeded, was applauded, and Sheridan begged her pardon. She described well the awe she felt, and the power of excitement given to her by the sight of Burke, Fox, Sheridan, and Sir Joshua Reynolds in the pit.

She invited us to a private reading-party at her own house; present, only her daughter (a very pretty young lady), a Mrs. Wilkinson, Mr. Burney, Dr. Holland, Lydia White, Mr. Harness, and ourselves. She read one of her finest parts, and that best suited to a private room— Queen Katherine. She was dressed so as to do well for the two parts she was to perform this night, of gentlewoman and queen,—black velvet, with black velvet cap and feathers. She sat the whole time, and with a large Shakespeare before her; as she knew the part of Katherine by heart, she seldom required the help of glasses, and she recited it incomparably well. The changes of her countenance were striking. From her first burst of indignation, when she objects to the cardinal as her judge, to her last expiring scene, all was so perfectly natural and so touching, we could give no applause but tears. Mrs. Siddons is beautiful even at this moment. Some who had seen her on the stage in this part assured me that it had a much greater effect upon them in a private room; because they were near enough to see the change in her countenance, and to hear the pathos of her half-suppressed voice. Some one said that, in the dying scene, her very pillow seemed sick.

She spoke afterwards of the different parts which she had liked and disliked to act; and, when she mentioned the characters and scenes she had found easy or difficult, it was curious to observe that the feelings of the actress and the

sentiments and reasons of the best critics meet.
Whatever was not natural, or inconsistent with
the main part of the character, she found she
could never act well.

———

SIR WALTER SCOTT TO MRS. MACLEAN CLEPHANE.

EDINBURGH, March 23, 1817.

. . . John Kemble is here to take leave, acting
over all his great characters, and with all the
spirit of his best years. He played *Coriolanus* last
night (the first time I have ventured out), fully
as well as I ever saw him ; and you know what
a complete model he is of the Roman.   He has
made a great reformation in his habits ; given
up wine, which he used to swallow by pailfuls
—and renewed his youth like the eagle's.   He
seems to me always to play best those characters in which there is a predominating tinge of
some overmastering passion, or acquired habit
of acting and speaking, coloring the whole man.
The patrician pride of *Coriolanus*, the stoicism
of *Brutus* and *Cato*, the rapid and hurried
vehemence of *Hotspur*, mark the class of characters I mean.   But he fails where a ready and
pliable yielding to the events and passions of
life makes what may be termed a more natural

personage. Accordingly I think his *Macbeth*, *Lear*, and especially his *Richard*, inferior in spirit and truth. In *Hamlet* the natural fixed melancholy of the prince places him within Kemble's range; yet many delicate and sudden turns of passion slip through his fingers. He is a lordly vessel, goodly and magnificent when going large before the wind, but wanting the facility to go "*ready about*," so that he is sometimes among the breakers before he can wear ship. Yet we lose in him a most excellent critic, an accomplished scholar, and one who graced our forlorn drama with what little it has left of good sense and gentlemanlike feeling. And so exit he. He made me write some lines to speak when he withdraws, and he has been here criticising and correcting till he got them quite to his mind, which has rather tired me.

THOMAS ROBINSON TO HENRY CRABB ROBINSON.

March 9, 1801.

. . . When we were in London, Mary and I had lodgings in Newgate Street. The theatre was the only amusement which interested me. We were, of course, desirous of seeing the present *nine days' wonder*, Mr. Cooke. We were so

lucky as to see him in *Richard*, his favorite
character. Nature has assisted him greatly in
the performance of this part—his features being
strongly marked and his voice harsh. I felt at
the time that he personated the ferocious
tyrant better than Kemble could have done.
There is besides a sort of humor in his manner
of acting which appeared very appropriate, and
which I think Kemble could not have given;
and I think it likely the latter would be sur-
passed in *Shylock*. Cooke's powers of expression are strong and coarse. I am persuaded
that in dignified and refined character—in the
philosophical hero—he would fall infinitely
short of Kemble. He had the effrontery to play
the "Stranger"; but, if I mistake not, he appeared in it but once. . . .

MRS. RICHARD TRENCH TO WILLIAM LEFAUN.

Bursledon Lodge, November 13, 1814.

You did me the honor to ask what I thought
of Kean. I saw him but once, and imperfectly,
being shut up, like a mouse in a telescope, in
one of the wretched private boxes, which savor
more of self-denial, penance, and privation, than
any views of pride or pleasure. . . . Yet he

delighted me in *Richard the Third.* He carries one's views forwards and backwards as to the character, instead of confining them, like other actors, within the limits of the present hour; and he gives a breadth of coloring to his part that strongly excites the imagination. He showed me that *Richard* possessed a mine of humor and pleasantry, with all the grace of high breeding grafted on strong and brilliant intellect. He gave probability to the drama by throwing this favorable light on the character, particularly in the scene with *Lady Anne;* and he made it more consistent with the varied lot of "poor humanity." He reminded me constantly of Bonaparte—that restless quickness, that Catiline inquietude, that fearful somewhat resembling the impatience of a lion in his cage. Though I am not a lover of the drama (will you despise me for the avowal?) I could willingly have heard him repeat his part that same evening.

CHARLES DICKENS TO ——

PARIS, February, 1855.

Incomparably the finest acting I ever saw, I saw last night at the Ambigu. They have revived that old piece, once immensely popular in London, under the name of *Thirty Years of a Gambler's Life.* Old Lemaitre plays his famous character, and never did I see any thing, in art, so exaltedly horrible and awful. In the earlier acts he was so well made up, and so light and active, that he really looked sufficiently young. But in the last two, when he had grown old and miserable, he did the finest things, I really believe, that are within the power of acting. Two or three times, a great cry of horror went all round the house. When he met, in the inn-yard, the traveller whom he murders, and first saw his money, the manner in which the crime came into his head—and eyes—was as truthful as it was terrific. This traveller, being a good fellow, gives him wine. You should see the dim remembrance of his better days that comes over him as he takes the glass, and in a strange dazed way makes as if he were going to touch the other man's, or do some airy thing with it ; and then stops and flings the contents down his hot throat, as if he were pouring it into a lime-kiln. But this was nothing to what follows after he has done the murder, and comes home, with a basket of provisions, a ragged pocket full of money, and a badly-washed bloody right hand—which his little girl finds out. After the child asked him if he had hurt his hand, his going aside, turning himself round, and looking over all his clothes for spots, was so inexpressibly dreadful that it really scared one. He called for wine, and the sickness that came upon him when he saw the color, was one of the things that brought out the curious cry I have spoken of, from the audience. Then he fell into a sort of bloody mist, and went on to the end groping about, with no mind for any thing, except making his fortune by staking this money, and a faint, dull kind of love for the child. It is quite impossible to satisfy one's self by saying enough of such a magnificent performance. I have never seen him come near its finest points, in any thing else. He said two things in a way that alone would put him far apart from all other actors. One to his wife, when he has exultingly shown her the money and she has asked him how he got it—" I found it "—and the other to his old companion and tempter, when he charged him with having killed that traveller, and he suddenly went head-long mad and took him by the throat and howled out : " It was n't I who murdered him

—it was Misery!" And such a dress; such a face; and, above all, such an extraordinary guilty wicked thing as he made of a knotted branch of a tree which was his walking-stick, from the moment when the idea of the murder came into his head! I could write pages about him. It is an impression quite ineffaceable. He got half-boastful of that walking-staff to himself, and half-afraid of it; and did n't know whether to be grimly pleased that it had the jagged end, or to hate it and be horrified at it. He sat at a little table in the inn-yard, drinking with the traveller; and this horrible stick got between them like the Devil, while he counted on his fingers the uses he could put the money to.

———

MRS. RICHARD TRENCH TO MRS. MARY LEADBEATER.

December 25, 1815.

You ask me of Mrs. Piozzi. She is a lively, animated woman, far advanced in years, and peculiarly agreeable in countenance, conversation, and manners. So she appeared to me, who have only met her in mixed company, and so I have heard her described by others. She is a woman of very high spirits, and only two

years ago went to a masquerade in Bath dis-
guised as a constable, Lady Belmore (the dow-
ager) and Miss Caldwell attending her as watch-
men ; and they amused themselves throwing
the whole assembly into consternation by pretending they had a warrant to disperse and im-
prison them as engaged in an illegal amusement.* . . .

CHARLES MATTHEWS TO HIS WIFE.

OSWESTRY, September 4, 1820.

The dear inseparable inimitables, Lady Buller and Miss Ponsonby, were in the boxes here
on Friday. They came twelve miles from
Llangollen, and returned, as they never sleep
from home. Oh, such curiosities ! I was nearly
convulsed. I could scarcely get on for the first
ten minutes after my eye caught them. Though
I had never seen them, I instantaneously knew
them. As they are seated, there is not one
point to distinguish them from men : the dressing and powdering of the hair ; their well-
starched neckcloths ; the upper part of their
habits, which they always wear, even at a dinner party, made precisely like men's coats ; and

* In 1815, Mrs. Piozzi was seventy-five years old. She died
in 1821.

regular black-beaver men's hats.   They looked
exactly like two respectable superannuated old
clergymen ; one the picture of Boruwlaski.   I
was highly flattered, as they never were in the
theatre before. . . .

———

JOHN GIBSON LOCKHART TO ——

ELLERAY, August 24, 1825.

. . . We slept on Wednesday evening at Ca-
pel Carig, which Sir W. supposes to mean the
Chapel of the Crags, a pretty little inn in a
most picturesque situation certainly, and as to
the matter of toasted cheese quite exquisite.
Next day we advanced through, I verily believe, the most perfect gem of a country eye
ever saw, having all the wildness of Highland
backgrounds, and all the loveliness of rich
English landscape nearer us, and streams like
the purest and most babbling of our own.   At
Llangollen your papa was waylaid by the celebrated " Ladies," viz.: Lady Eleanor Buller
and the Honorable Miss Ponsonby, who having been one or both crossed in love, foreswore
all dreams of matrimony in the heyday of
youth, beauty, and fashion, and selected this
charming spot for the repose of their now time-

honored virginity. It was many a day, however, before they could get implicit credit for
being the innocent friends they really were
among the people of the neighborhood, for
their elopement from Ireland had been performed under suspicious circumstances, and as
Lady Eleanor arrived here in her natural aspect
of a pretty girl, while Miss Ponsonby had con-
descended to accompany her in the garb of a
smart footman in buckskin breeches, years and
years elapsed ere full justice was done to the
character of their romance. We proceeded up
the hill, and found every thing about them and
their habitation odd and extravagant beyond
report. Imagine two women, one apparently
seventy, the other sixty-five, dressed in heavy
blue riding-habits, enormous shoes, and men's
hats, with their petticoats so tucked up that at
the first glance of them, fussing and tottering
about their porch in the agony of expectation,
we took them for a couple of hazy or crazy old
sailors. On nearer inspection, they both wear
a world of brooches, rings, etc., and Lady
Eleanor positively *orders*—several stars and
crosses, and a red ribbon, exactly like a K. C.
B. To crown all, they have crop heads, shaggy,

rough, bushy, and as white as snow, the one
with age alone, the other assisted by a sprink-
ling of powder. The elder lady is almost
blind, and every way much decayed; the
other, the ci-devant groom, in good preservation. But who could paint the prints, the dogs,
the cats, the miniatures, the cram of cabinets,
clocks, glass-cases, books, bijouterie, dragon-
china, nodding mandarins, and whirligigs of
every shape and hue—the whole house outside and in (for we must see every thing in the
dressing closets), *covered* with carved oak, very
rich and fine some of it—and the illustrated
copies of Sir W.'s poems, and the joking, sim-
pering compliments about Waverley, and the
anxiety to know who MacIvor really was, and
the absolute devouring of the poor Unknown,
who had to carry off, besides all the rest, one
small bit of literal *butter* dug up in a Milesian
stone jar lately from the bottom of some Irish
bog. Great romance, *i. e.*, absurd innocence of
character, one must have looked for; but it
was confounding to find this mixed up with
such eager curiosity, and enormous knowledge
of the tattle and scandal of the world they had
so long left. Their tables were plied with
newspapers from every corner of the kingdom,

and they seemed to have the deaths and marriages of the antipodes at their fingers' ends. Their albums and autographs, from Louis XVIII. and George IV., down to magazine poets and quack-doctors, are a museum. I shall never see the spirit of blue-stockingism again in such perfect incarnation. Peveril won't get over their final kissing match for a week. Yet it is too bad to laugh at these good old girls ; they have long been the guardian angels of the village, and are worshipped by man, woman, and child about them.

THOMAS CARLYLE TO HIS BROTHER.

CHELSEA, April 16, 1839.

. . . I must tell you of the strangest compliment of all, which occurred since I wrote last—the advent of Count d'Orsay. About a fortnight ago this Phœbus Apollo of dandyism, escorted by poor little Chorley, came whirling hither in a chariot that struck all Chelsea into mute amazement with splendor. Chorley's under jaw went like the hopper or under riddle of a pair of fanners, such was his terror on bringing such a splendor into actual contact with such a grimness. Nevertheless, we did amazingly well, the Count and I. He is a tall fellow

of six feet three, built like a tower, with floods
of dark-auburn hair, with a beauty, with an
adornment unsurpassable on this planet ; withal
a rather substantial fellow at bottom, by no
means without insight, without fun, and a sort
of rough sarcasm rather striking out of such a
a porcelain figure. He said, looking at Shel-
ley's bust, in his French accent : " Ah, it is one
of those faces who weesh to swallow their
chin." He admired the fine epic, etc., etc. ;
hoped I would call soon, and see Lady Bless-
ington withal. Finally he went his way, and
Chorley with reassumed jaw. Jane laughed for
two days at the contrast of my plaid dress-
ing-gown, bilious, iron countenance, and this
Paphian apparition. I did not call till the other
day, and left my card merely. I do not see
well what good I can get by meeting him
much, or Lady B. and demirepdom, though I
should not object to see it once, and then of-
tener, if agreeable. . . .

MISS MARIA EDGEWORTH TO ——

PARIS, 1802.

. . . You know the Parisian houses are inhab-
ited by hordes of different people, and the stairs

are in fact streets, to their dwellings. The porter,
who was neither obliging nor intelligent, carelessly said that "*Madame de Genlis logeait au
seconde à gauche, qu'il faudrait tirer sa sonnette*"
—he believed she was at home if she was not
gone out. . . . The door was opened by a
girl of about Honora's size, holding an ill-set-
up, wavering candle in her hand, the light of
which fell upon her face and figure. Her face
was remarkably intelligent, dark, sparkling eyes,
dark hair, curled in the most fashionable long
corkscrew ringlets over her eyes and cheeks.
She parted the ringlets to take a full view of
us, and we were equally impatient to take a full
view of her. The dress of her figure by no means
suited the head and the elegance of her attitude. What her "nether weeds" might be we
could not distinctly see, but they seemed to be
a coarse, short petticoat, like what Molly Bristol's children wear, not on Sundays; a woollen
gray spencer above, pinned with a single pin by
the lapels tight across the neck under the chin,
and open all below. After surveying us and
hearing that our name was Edgeworth, she
smiled graciously and bid us follow her, saying,
"*Maman est chez elle.*" She led the way with

the grace of a young lady who has been taught
to dance, across two ante-chambers, miserable-
looking, but miserable or not, no house in Paris
can be without them.   The girl or young lady,
for we were still in doubt which to think her,
led us into a small room, in which the candles
were so well screened by a green tin screen that
we could scarcely distinguish the tall form of
a lady in black who rose from her arm-chair by
the fireside as the door opened : a great puff of
smoke came from the huge fireplace at the same
moment. She came forward, and we made our
way towards her as well as we could through a
confusion of tables, chairs, and work-baskets,
china, writing-desks, and inkstands, and bird-
cages, and a harp. She did not speak, and as her
back was now turned to both fire and candle I
could not see her face, nor any thing but the
outline of her form and her attitude. Her form
was the remains of a fine form, and her attitude
that of a woman used to a better drawing-
room. I, being foremost, and she silent, was
compelled to speak to the figure in darkness :
" *Madame de Genlis nous a fait l'honneur de
nous mander qu'elle voulait bien nous permettre
de lui rendre visite, et de lui offrir nos respects,*"

said I, or words to that effect; to which she replied by taking my hand, and saying something
in which "*charmée*" was the most intelligible
word. Whilst she spoke she looked over my
shoulder at my father, whose bow, I presume,
told her he was a gentleman, for she spoke to
him immediately as if she wished to please, and
seated us in fauteuils near the fire. I then had
a full view of her face and figure. She looked
like the full-length picture of my great-grand-
mother Edgeworth you may have seen in the
garret, very thin and melancholy, but her face
not so handsome as my grandmother's; dark
eyes, long sallow cheeks, compressed thin lips,
two or three black ringlets on a high forehead,
a cap that Mrs. Grier might wear—altogether
an appearance of fallen fortunes, worn-out
health, and excessive but guarded irritability.
To me there was nothing of that engaging, cap-
tivating manner which I had been taught to
expect by many even of her enemies. She
seemed to me to be alive only to literary quar-
rels and jealousies; the muscles of her face as
she spoke, or my father spoke to her, quickly
and too easily expressed hatred and anger
whenever any not of her own party were men-

tioned.   She is now, you know, *devote acharnée.*
When I mentioned with some enthusiasm the
good Abbé Marellet, who has written so cour-
ageously in favor of the French exiled nobility
and their children, she answered in a sharp
voice :   " *Oui, c'est un homme de beaucoup
d'esprit, à ce qu'on je crois meme, mais il faut
apprendre qu'il n'est pas des Notres.*"   . . .   She
spoke of Madame de Staël's " Delphine " with
detestation ; of another new and fashionable
novel, " Amélie," with abhorrence, and kissed
my forehead twice because I had not read it ;
" *Vous autres Anglaises, vous etes modestes !* "
Where was Madame de Genlis' sense of delicacy
when she penned and published " Les Chevaliers
du Cigne " ? Forgive, my dear Aunt Mary. You
begged me to see with favorable eyes, and I
went to see her after seeing her " Rosière de Sa-
lency," with the most favorable disposition, but
I could not like her.   There was something of
malignity in her countenance and conversation
that repelled love, and of hypocrisy which an-
nihilated esteem ; and from time to time I saw,
or thought I saw, through the gloom of her
countenance, a gleam of coquetry. But my
father judges much more favorably of her than

I do. She evidently took pains to please him, and he says he is sure she is a person over whose mind he could gain great ascendancy. He thinks her a woman of violent passions, unbridled imagination, and ill-tempered, but not malevolent; one who has been so torn to pieces that she now turns upon her enemies, and longs to tear in her turn. He says she has certainly great powers of pleasing, though I certainly neither saw nor felt them. . . .

CHARLES DICKENS TO ——

EDINBURGH, June, 1841.

. . . Walking up and down the hall of the courts of law (which was full of advocates, writers to the signet, clerks, and idlers) was a tall, burly, handsome man of eight and fifty, with a gait like O'Connell's, the bluest eye you can imagine, and long hair—longer than mine— falling down in a wild way under the broad brim of his hat. He had on a surtout coat, a blue checked shirt, the collar standing up, and kept in its place with a wisp of black necker- chief; no waistcoat; and a large pocket-hand- kerchief thrust into his breast, which was all broad and open. At his heels followed a wiry,

sharp-eyed, shaggy devil of a terrier, dogging
his steps as he went slashing up and down, now
with one man beside him, now with another,
and now quite alone, but always at a fast, roll-
ing pace, with his head in the air, and his eyes
as wide open as he could get them. I guessed
it was Wilson, and it was. A bright, clear-
complexioned, mountain-looking fellow, he
looks as though he had just come down from
the Highlands, and had never in his life taken
pen in hand. But he has had an attack of
paralysis in his right arm, within this month.
He winced when I shook hands with him ; and
once or twice, when we were walking up and
down, slipped as if he had stumbled on a piece
of orange-peel. He is a great fellow to look
at, and to talk to; and, if you could divest
your mind of the actual Scott, is just the figure
you would put in his place. . . .

MRS. ANNE GRANT TO MRS. HOOK.

EDINBURGH, February 26, 1817.

. . . You ask me to tell you about Dr. Chalmers. I must tell you first, then, that of all
men he is the most modest, and speaks with
undissembled gentleness and liberality of those

who differ from him in opinion. Every word
he says has the stamp of genius, yet the calmness, ease, and simplicity of his conversation is
such, that to ordinary minds he might appear
an ordinary man. I had a great intellectual
feast about three weeks since. I breakfasted
with him at a friend's house, and enjoyed his
society for two hours with great delight. Conversation wandered into various channels, but
he was always powerful, always gentle, and always seemed quite unconscious of his own
superiority. I had not been an hour at home
when a guest arrived who had become a stranger to me for some time past. It was Walter
Scott, who sat a long time with me, and was,
as he always is, delightful; his good nature,
good humor, and simplicity are truly charming;
you never once think of his superiority, because
it is evident he does not think of it himself.
He, too, confirmed the maxim that true genius
is ever modest and careless; after his greatest
literary triumphs he is like Hardyknute's son
after a victory, when we are told,—

> " With careless gesture, mind unmov'd,
>   On rode he ow're the plain."

Mary and I could not help observing certain

similarities between these two extraordinary persons (Chalmers and Scott): the same quiet, unobtrusive humor, the same flow of rich original conversation, easy, careless, and visibly unpremeditated; the same indulgence for others, and readiness to give attention and interest to any subject started by others. There was a more chastened dignity and occasional elevation in the Divine than in the Poet, but many resembling features in their modes of thinking and manner of expression. . . .

MISS MARIA LEYCESTER TO MISS HIBBERT.

STOKE RECTORY, October 24, 1819.

I have not yet told you of the pleasantest part of our tour, our visit to Sir Walter Scott. He lives about three miles from Melrose, and our first day's journey from Edinburgh was to his house. We had a letter to him from Reginald Heber, and Mr. Scott persuaded us to stay three days with him, during which time we had full opportunity of becoming acquainted with him. We were the only strangers, and therefore had his conversation all to ourselves, and most highly were we gratified. He is un-affected and simple in his manner to the greatest degree, and at first his countenance only speaks good humor; but mention any subject that interests him, and he lights up in an instant into fire and animation. He is a kind of person one could not feel afraid of for a moment. Whatever subject you begin is the same to him; he has something entertaining to tell of every one, and the quickness with which he catches up every thing that is passing, even at the other end of the room, is surprising. His family consists of a very insignificant little wife, a French woman, quite inferior to him, and his daughters, who are fine, sensible, clever girls, quite brought up by him. The eldest sang Jacobite songs and border ballads to us with such spirit and enthusiasm, that it was delightful, and their love for Scotland makes them quite worthy of it. Their chief delight is in the border stories and traditions, in which they are very rich. His house is built by himself, and is very odd and picturesque. . . .

CHARLES ROBERT LESLIE TO HIS SISTER.

LONDON, June 28, 1850.

When I last wrote, I was about to be introduced to Sir Walter Scott. He quite answered all my expectations of him, and you may suppose they were very high. His manners are those of an amiable and unaffected man, and a polished gentleman, and his conversation is something higher, for it is often quite as amusing and interesting as his novels, and without any apparent attempt at display. It flows from him in the most easy and natural manner. As I take it for granted that the most insignificant particulars relating to such a man will be interesting to you, I will give you a description of his personal appearance, and even his dress. He is tall and well formed, excepting one of his ankles and feet (I think the right) which is crippled, and makes him walk very lamely. He is neither fat nor thin. His face is perfectly Scotch, and though some people think it heavy, it struck me as a very agreeable one. He never could have been handsome. His forehead is very high, his nose short, his upper lip long, and the lower part of his face rather fleshy. His complexion is fresh and clear, his eyes very blue, shrewd, and penetrating. I should say the predominant expression of his face is that of strong sense. His hair, which has always been very light (as well as his eyebrows and eyelashes), is now of a silvery whiteness, which makes him look somewhat older than he really is (I believe forty-six is his age).* . . .

———

MISS MARIA EDGEWORTH TO ——

EDINBURGH, June, 1823.

. . . We were tired, not fit to be seen; but I thought it right to accept Walter Scott's cordial invitation,† sent for a hackney-coach, and, just as we were, without dressing, went. As the coach stopped, we saw the hall lighted, and the moment the door opened, heard the joyous sounds of loud singing. Three servants " the Miss Edgeworths " sounded from hall to landing-place ; and, as I paused for a moment in the ante-room, I heard the first sound of Walter Scott's voice—" The Miss Edgeworths *come !* "

* Scott was nearly forty-nine at this time.

† Sir Walter Scott had written a very cordial letter, with the following postscript :

" My wife insists I shall add that the Laird of Staffa promised to look in on us this evening at eight or nine, for the purpose of letting us hear one of his clansmen sing some Highland boat-songs, and the like ; and that if you will come, as the Irish should to the Scotch, without any ceremony, you will hear what is more curious than mellifluous. The man returns to the Isles to-morrow. There are no strangers with us, no party ; none but all our own family, and two old friends."

The room was lighted by only one globe lamp. A circle were singing loud and beating time : all stopped in an instant ; and Sir Walter Scott, in the most cordial and courteous manner, stepped forward to welcome us: " Miss Edgeworth, this is so kind of you ! "

My first impression was that he was neither so large nor so heavy in appearance as I had been led to expect by description, prints, bust, and picture. He is more lame than I expected, but not unwieldy. His countenance, even by the uncertain light in which I first saw it, pleased me much : benevolent and full of genius, without the slightest effort at expression ; delightfully natural, as if he did not know he was Walter Scott, or the Great Unknown of the North ; as if he only thought of making others happy. After naming to us " Lady Scott, Staffa, my daughter Lockhart, Sophia, another daughter Anne, my son, my son-in-law Lockhart," just in the broken circle as they then stood, and showing me that only his family and two friends, Mr. Clarke and Mr. Sharpe, were present, he sat down for a moment on a low sofa ; and, on my saying, " Do not let us interrupt what was going on," he immediately rose and begged

Staffa to bid his boatman strike up again. "Will you then join in the circle with us?"— he put the end of a silk handkerchief into my hand, and others into my sister's. They held by these handkerchiefs all in their circle again ; and the boatman began to roar out a Gaelic song, to which they all stamped in time, and repeated a chorus, which, as far as I could hear, sounded like "*At am Vaun! at am Vaun!*" frequently repeated with prodigious enthusiasm. In another I could make out no intelligible sound but "Bar! bar! bar!" But the boat-man's dark eyes were ready to start out of his head with rapture as he sang and stamped, and shook the handkerchief on each side, and the circle imitated.

Lady Scott is so exactly what I have seen her described, that it seemed as if we had seen her before. She must have been very handsome— French, dark, large eyes, civil, and good-natured.

Supper at a round table—a family supper— with attention to us just sufficient, and no more. The impression left on my mind this night was that Walter Scott is one of the best-bred men I ever saw, with all the exquisite politeness, which he knows so well how to describe, which is of no particular school or country, but which is of all countries—the politeness which arises from good and quick sense and feeling, which seems to know by instinct the character of others, to see what will please, and put all his guests at their ease. As I sat beside him at supper I could not believe he was a stranger, and forgot he was a great man. . . .

SIR WALTER SCOTT TO MISS JOANNA BAILLIE.

Edinburgh, July 11, 1823.

We saw, you will readily suppose, a great deal of Miss Edgeworth, and two very nice girls, her younger sisters. It is scarcely possible to say more of this very remarkable person than that she not only completely answered, but exceeded, the expectations which I had formed. I am particularly pleased with the *naïveté* and good-humored ardor of mind which she unites with such formidable powers of acute observation. In external appearance she is quite the fairy of our nursery tale,—the Whippity Stourie, if you remember such a sprite, who came flying through the window to work all sorts of marvels. I will never believe but what she has a wand in her pocket, and pulls it out to conjure a little before she begins to draw those very striking pictures of manners. . . .

THOMAS BABINGTON MACAULAY TO HIS MOTHER.

COURT HOUSE, POMFRET, April 15, 1828.

. . . My Edinburgh expedition has given me so much to say that, unless I write off some of it before I come home, I shall talk you all to death, and be voted a bore in every house which I visit. I will commence with Jeffrey himself. I had almost forgotten his person: and, indeed, I should not wonder if even now I were to forget it again. He has twenty faces almost as unlike each other as my father's to Mr. Wilberforce's, and infinitely more unlike to each other than those of near relatives often are ; infinitely more unlike, for example, than those of the two Grants. When absolutely quiescent, reading a paper, or hearing a conversation in which he takes no interest, his countenance shows no indication whatever of intellectual superiority of any kind. But as soon as he is interested, and opens his eyes upon you, the change is like magic. There is a flash in his glance, a violent contortion in his frown, an exquisite humor in his sneer, and a sweetness

and brilliancy in his smile, beyond any thing
that ever I witnessed.   A person who had seen
him in only one state would not know him if
he saw him in another. For he has not, like
Brougham, marked features which in all moods
of mind remain unaltered. The mere outline
of his face is insignificant. The expression is
every thing; and such power and variety of expression I never saw in any human countenance, not even in that of the most celebrated
actors.   I can conceive that Garrick may have
been like him.   I have seen several pictures of
Garrick, none resembling another, and I have
heard Hannah More speak of the extraordinary
variety of countenance by which he was distinguished, and of the unequalled radiance and
penetration of his eye. The voice and delivery
of Jeffrey resemble his face. He possesses considerable power of mimicry, and rarely tells a
story without imitating several different ac-
cents. His familiar tone, his declamatory tone,
and his pathetic tone are quite different things.
Sometimes Scotch predominates in his pronunciation; sometimes it is imperceptible.
Sometimes his utterance is snappish and quick
to the last degree ; sometimes it is remarkable

for rotundity and mellowness. I can easily conceive that two people who had seen him on different days might dispute about him as the travellers in the fable disputed about the chameleon.

In one thing, as far as I observed, he is always the same ; and that is the warmth of his domestic affections. Neither Mr. Wilberforce nor my uncle Babington comes up to him in this respect. The flow of his kindness is quite inexhaustible. Not five minutes pass without some fond expression or caressing gesture to his wife or his daughter. He has fitted up a study for himself: but he never goes into it. Law papers, reviews, whatever he has to write, he writes in the drawing-room or in his wife's boudoir. When he goes to other parts of the country on a retainer he takes them in the carriage with him. I do not wonder that he should be a good husband ; for his wife is a very amiable woman. But I was surprised to see a man so keen and sarcastic, so much of a scoffer, pouring himself out with such simplicity and tenderness in all sorts of affectionate nonsense. Through our whole journey to Perth he kept up a sort of mock quarrel with his daughter; at-

tacked her about novel-reading, laughed her
into a pet, kissed her out of it, and laughed her
into it again.   She and her mother absolutely
idolize him, and I do not wonder at it.

His conversation is very much like his countenance and his voice, of immense variety;
sometimes plain and unpretending even to flat-
ness; sometimes whimsically brilliant and
rhetorical almost beyond the license of private
discourse. He has many interesting anecdotes,
and tells them very well. He is a shrewd ob-
server; and so fastidious that I am not surprised
at the awe in which many people seem to stand
when in his company. Though not altogether
free from affectation himself, he has a peculiar
loathing for it in other people, and a great
talent for discovering and exposing it.   He has
a particular contempt, in which I most heartily
concur with him, for the *fadaises* of blue-stock-
ing literature, for the mutual flatteries of
coteries, the handing about of *vers de société*,
the albums, the conversaziones, and all the other
nauseous trickeries of the Sewards, Hayleys,
and Sothebys.   I am not quite sure that he has
escaped the opposite extreme, and that he is
not a little too desirous to appear rather a man

of the world, an active lawyer, or an easy careless gentleman, than a distinguished writer. I
must own that when Jeffrey and I were by ourselves, he talked much and very well on literary
topics. His kindness and hospitality to me
were, indeed, beyond description : and his wife
was as pleasant and friendly as possible. I
liked every thing but the hours. We were never
up till ten, and never retired till two hours at
least after midnight. Jeffrey, indeed, never
goes to bed till sleep comes on him overpower-
ingly, and never rises till forced up by business
or hunger. He is extremely well in health ; so
that I could not help suspecting him of being
very hypochondriac ; for all his late letters to me
have been filled with lamentations about his
various maladies. His wife told me, when I
congratulated her on his recovery, that I must
not absolutely rely on all his accounts of his
own diseases. I really think that he is, on the
whole, the youngest-looking man of fifty that I
know, at least when he is animated. . . .

DANIEL MACMILLAN TO JAMES MACLEHOSE.

LONDON, June 4, 1840.

. . . What do you think? I have been to
one of Carlyle's lectures ; my brother Alexander

has been to another. . . . Have you seen the portrait by Count D'Orsay? That is an excellent likeness. He lectures without notes of any kind, having thrown aside even the piece of paper like a visiting card, which he used to bring with him. He is very far from being a fluent speaker. Sometimes he rises into eloquence and gets applauded; sometimes he comes to a dead stand for want of a word, quietly looking in the face of his audience till he finds the word; sometimes he leaves his sentences in a quite unfinished state, and passes on to something else, *e. g.*, speaking of the difference between Dante's time and ours, he said, " *Our* highest has become unattainably high. The apex "—here came a dead stop for three or four moments, and at last, not being able to complete his sentence, he goes on to say, " *Our* universe has everywhere expanded itself," etc., etc. He rarely moves his hands from the sides of his desk. When he does, it is to rub his two forefingers along his forehead, just above his eyebrows. This seems to be of great use, enabling him to get on much better, at least I suppose so, because he always said his best things after one or two of these rubs.

His whole appearance and manner is exceedingly simple. I never saw any one so completely free from any thing like pretension. His accent and pronunciation is very broad Scotch, much more so, I think, than Dr. Chalmers'. His dress is plain and simple enough, but no way remarkable. . . .

———

THOMAS GUTHRIE TO HIS WIFE.

LONDON, February 17, 1856.

. . . I did not wish to disturb Mr. Carlyle, but he came, and an uncommon-looking man he is; an eagle-like look in his great glaring eyes, hair half gray, and a strong Dumfrieshire tongue. He was in a *robe de chambre*, most kind and courteous. I got him upon the neglect of the uneducated and lapsed classes; he and I were quite at one. He uttered a number of great thoughts in magnificent language; lightened and thundered away in sublime style—at the heads of governors, ladies and gentlemen, and this selfish world; and looked to me very much, as he swung his arm, clenched his fist, and glared round him with his black beard and shining eyes and grizzley hair, like an incarnation of Thor, or Woden, or some other Scandinavian divinity. . . .

PORTOBELLO, 1856.

. . . We spent some hours with Carlyle two
or three days ago as he passed through Edinburgh, and went as far as Granton with him on
his way to Fife. You should have seen the looks
of the people in the train as he rolled forth
(swaying to and fro the while, with the restless-
ness of some wild creature) the most idiosyn-
cratic denunciations of railways, nineteenth
centuries, steam-engines, cheap literature,
" clever " people, and civilization generally.
Though of course they had no notion of who
he was, he gradually got them into a sort of
mesmeric possession that stilled every voice but
his own and stretched every eye. . . . In the
midst of all this thunderous lava he was very
kind and sweet to us, and his last words to
E—— were a spontaneous assurance that he
would seek us out when he returned from the
North. All of his face that his moustache and
thick beard left bare had a ruddy health upon
it which contrasted pleasantly with his morbid
London looks, and which showed that the weeks
in the moorlands near which he was born
(" covered in with solitude and silence," and

out of reach of any human being that knew
him), where he had just, he declared, been
spending the "most altogether blessed days he
could remember," had been of more than mental benefit. . . .

MRS. ANNE GRANT TO MRS. GORMAN.

DUNBLANE, September 24, 1819.

. . . The morning before we left Edinburgh
we had the Laureate * to breakfast, that being
the only time he could afford to us. I had
James Wilson to meet him, a younger and
graver brother of John Wilson, of the "Isle of
Palms." When I speak of gravity, I mean the
grave countenance with which he says things
irresistibly ludicrous; he is, in fact, the author
of some of the best, at least the most refined
wit in *Blackwood's Magazine.* But to return
to the Laureate, I like him exceedingly; he has
the finest poetical countenance, features unusu-
ally high, and somewhat strong though regular;
a quantity of bushy black hair, worn carelessly,
but not with affected negligence; deep-set, but
very animated black eyes; and a countenance
serious and collected, but kindling into ardor

* Southey.

when animated in conversation. I have heard Southey called silent and constrained; I did not find him so; he talked easily and much, without seeming in the least consequential, or saying a single word for effect. On the contrary, he converses with the feeling and earnestness of one who speaks, not to flourish in conversation, but to relieve a full mind from subjects of frequent meditation. . . .

DANIEL MACMILLAN TO DAVID WATT.

LONDON, September 29, 1842.

I intended to have commenced a letter to you immediately after my return from Hurtsmonceaux, giving you an account of my visit, what I saw and heard. But something or other came, day by day, ever since to hinder me, and here at last I must write hurriedly, so the less time I spend in apologies the better. . . . The foremost figure is, of course, the Archdeacon himself.* He is about six feet, not at all stout, not very slender. Something like Mr. Binney as to height, not at all like him otherwise. His eye is large, soft, swimming, not dark-blue, nor gray, nor hazel, but a sort of mixture of these.

* Julius Hare.

His hair was dark, but is now copiously sprinkled with gray. His complexion is rather sallow; his forehead broad and rather, but not very, high. He takes no care to show his forehead, as his grizzled hair lies carelessly about his temples. His expression is that of a very thoughtful, kind-hearted, simple-minded man, quite free from all self-consciousness. I never met so humble-minded a man. He stoops a little, the result of too much reading, I should think. He is very frank, and I felt quite at ease with him. His only brother, Marcus, who was a captain in the navy, was there, with his wife and three children. The widow of his brother Augustus was also there, with her only child, a boy about seven. They were all very pleasant people. I felt quite at home with them. Their easy good-breeding made me feel so. They talked with freedom and ease on all sorts of subjects—and yet they were far from being great talkers, a very disgusting kind of people to me.

I wish I could give you any thing like a notion of the conversation—but that is impossible.

Landor had been there about a week before me. If I had gone when I was first asked, I should have met him. From all the Hares say, and they know Landor well, and have known him for many years, there is little chance of his ever producing the " Solid and Orderly work on History," of which he speaks in the preface to his *Conversations.* He is so full of strange perversions and unrest. He is a noble, warmhearted man ; but quite devoid of any thing like philosophical or judicial calmness, and seems to get more and more excitable as his years increase. Nothing delights him more than to pester his visitors, or his host, or any one he meets in company, with all manner of paradoxes. The truly amiable and lovely nature of Tiberius, or of Nero ; or the great folly or cruelty of Pitt and Fox; or an examination of the question which of the two (Fox or Pitt) was the greater fool—always deciding in favor of Fox—for he, according to Landor, was the greatest fool of his day. Pitt, he says, was fool enough, but had a little of the rogue. Sometimes he discourses on the grandeur and beauty and harmony of the modern Greek and Latin prize poems of Oxford and Cambridge; showing them to be in every way superior to all that the Greeks or the Romans ever wrote! Or perhaps he spends an hour in proving that Monckton Milnes is the greatest English poet. In these humors he praises what others blame, and abuses whatever is well spoken of. . . .

———

MISS MARY ALEXANDER TO MARIA HARE.

HURTSMONCEAUX, August 15, 1852.

The dear Archdeacon * is better than when we wrote last; during these beautiful days he has been out a good deal in the garden, and though he comes in exhausted, still the quiet morning in the open air is good for him. Landor's visit has been a great enjoyment to the host, and still more so to the hostess, for I never saw Esther so animated, so amused, so drawn out. The mental vigor and effluence of Landor is indeed surprising. He gave his rich stores without stint, and was so gentle and well-bred that he seemed more pleased to receive than to bestow. He was occupied all day by his books, pen, or walking, and claimed not a moment of anybody's time; but you may suppose there was a beautiful display of summer lightning at breakfast, dinner, and in the evening! Bunsen's visit you will have heard of—

* Julius Hare.

curious contrast of minds and habits ! I watched the two as they walked to and fro in the garden, sometimes standing still in the earnestness of discussion ; Bunsen with all the action and vivacity of demonstration, Landor like a block of granite, immovable and apparently unimpressible. . . .

———

ROBERT SOUTHEY TO GROSVENOR C. BEDFORD.

KESWICK, April 26, 1808.

. . . At Bristol I met with a man of all others whom I was desirous of meeting—the only man living of whose praise I was ambitious, or whose censure would have humbled me. You will be curious to know who this could be. Savage Landor, the author of " Gebir," a poem which, unless you have heard me speak of it, you have probably never heard of at all. I never saw any one more unlike myself in every prominent part of human character, nor any one who so cordially and instinctively agreed with me on so many of the most important subjects. I have often said, before we met, that I would walk forty miles to see him, and, having seen him, I would gladly walk fourscore to see him again. He talked of " Thalaba," and I told him of the series of mythological poems which I had planned—mentioned some of the leading incidents on which they were to have been formed, and also told him for what reason they were laid aside—in plain English, that I could not afford to write them. Landor's reply was: "Go on with them, and I will pay for printing them, as many as you will write, and as many copies as you please." I had reconciled myself to my abdication (if the phrase may be allowable), and am not sure that this princely offer has not done me mischief; for it has awakened in me old dreams and hopes which had been laid aside, and a stinging desire to go on, for the sake of showing him poem after poem, and saying: "I need not accept your offer, but I have done this because you made it." It is something to be praised by one's peers; ordinary praise I regard as little as ordinary abuse. God bless you!

SIR EDWARD BULWER LYTTON TO LADY BLESS-INGTON.

NAPLES, November 26, 1834 (?).

. . . While I thank you for your introduction to Sir William Gell, I ought not to forget that to Landor, who was particularly kind to me, and whom I liked exceedingly. One is at home instantly with men of real genius; their oddities, their humors, don't put one out half as much as the formal regularity of your half-clever prigs. But Landor, thanks to your introduction, had no humors, no oddities for me. He invited me to his villa, which is charmingly situated, and smoothed himself down so much that I thought him one of the best-bred men I ever met, as well as one of the most really able (pity, nevertheless, so far as his talent is concerned, that he pets paradoxes so much; he keeps them as other people keep dogs—coaxes them, plays with them, and now and then sets them to bite a disagreeable intruder). . . .

THOMAS CARLYLE TO RALPH WALDO EMERSON.

LONDON, April 1, 1840.

. . . Of Landor I have not got much benefit either. We met first, some four years ago, on Cheyne Walk here: a tall, broad, burly man, with gray hair, and large, fierce-rolling eyes; of the most restless, impetuous vivacity, not to be held in by the most perfect breeding,—expressing itself in high-colored superlatives, indeed in reckless exaggeration, now and then in a dry,

sharp laugh, not of sport but of mockery; a
wild man, whom no extent of culture had been
able to tame! His intellectual faculty seemed
to me to be weak in proportion to his violence
of temper: the judgment he gives about any
thing is more apt to be wrong than right,—as
the inward whirlwind shows him this side or the
other of the object; and *sides* of an object are
all that he sees. . . . He visits London in
May; but says always it would kill him soon:
alas, I can well believe that! They say he has
a kind heart; nor does it seem unlikely: a perfectly honest heart, free and fearless, dwelling
amid such hallucinations, excitations, tempestu-
ous confusions, I can see he has. Enough of
him! Me he likes well enough, more thanks to
him; but two hours of such speech as his leave
me giddy and undone. . . .

———

MRS. FELICIA DOROTHEA HEMANS TO ——

RYDAL MOUNT, June 22, 1830.

. . . I felt very forlorn after you were gone
from Ambleside: —— came and went without
exciting a smile, and my nervous fear at the idea
of presenting myself alone to Mr. Wordsworth
grew upon me so rapidly that it was more than

seven before I took the courage to leave the
inn. I had, indeed, little cause for such trepidation. I was driven to a lovely, cottage-like
building, almost hidden by a profusion of roses
and ivy, and a most benignant-looking old man
greeted me in the porch. This was Mr. Wordsworth himself, and when I tell you that, having
rather a large party of visitors in the house, he
led me to a room apart from them, and brought
in his family by degrees, I am sure that little
trait will give you an idea of considerate kindness which you will both like and appreciate.
In half an hour I felt myself as much at ease
with him as I had been with Sir Walter Scott
in half a day. I laughed to find myself saying,
on the occasion of some little domestic occur-
rence : " Mr. Wordsworth, how *could* you be so
giddy ? " He has, undeniably, a lurking love of
mischief, and would not, I think, be half so
safely entrusted with the tied-up bag of winds
as Mr. —— insisted that Dr. Channing might
be. There is an almost patriarchal simplicity,
and an absence of all pretension about him,
which I know you would like ; all is free, unstudied, " the river winding at its own sweet
will." In his manner and conversation there is

more of impulse than I had expected, but, in other respects, I see much that I should look for in the poet of meditative life; frequently his head droops, his eyes half-close, and he seems buried in great depths of thought. I have passed a delightful morning to-day in walking with him about his own richly-shaded grounds, and hearing him speak of the old English writers, particularly Spenser, whom he loves, as he himself expresses it, for his " earnestness and his devotedness." It is an immeasurable transition from Spenser to ——, but I have been so much amused by Mr. Wordsworth's characterizing her as " a tumultuous young woman," that I cannot forbear transcribing the expression for the use of my friends.

BENJAMIN ROBERT HAYDON TO MISS MARY RUSSELL MITFORD.

May 31, 1842.

. . . On Tuesday Wordsworth breakfasted with us alone and went to church, and afterwards to Lockhart, who took us to the Zoölogical—as a part of the wild beasts. Wordsworth's silver-haired simplicity contrasted with Lockhart's arch mischief, and was exquisite. Wordsworth sat down to rest and told us a delightful story, so beautifully, as if an Apostle was unbending. I looked up and saw Lockhart relishing the whole thing, as if for a moment bewitched out of his melancholy mocking. What an expression I caught then for one of my Cartoons! So when you see it, remember. The story was this: A friend of Gainsborough's had a sweet child who was going away to school. As her father was on a sick-bed he was touched at parting with her. This came to Gainsborough's ears. So Gainsborough looked out for her, and said to her: "My little love, can you keep a secret?" "I don't know," said she, "but I 'll try." "Well," said he, "you come to me to-morrow." She came, and he painted her portrait, in order that when she was gone it might be placed at the foot of papa's bed, to delight him. The child went to school enjoying her secret, and the next morning, when her father opened his eyes, there was the image of his darling looking at him from the bottom of his bed!

You never heard any human being tell such a simple story so touchingly. It would have softened the hearts of the lions and tigers could they have heard it.

As Wordsworth was telling this in a shady
nook, I sitting by him, Lockhart before us
standing, and looking complacently down, the
sun shone on Wordsworth's silvery hairs, while
his dull eyes, with that look of internal vision I
never saw in any other face, told of thought
unknown to any but his Maker—out of the
window came the long neck and calm, large-
eyed head of the camelopard, as if above all
human anxiety, and with an air of quiescent
contempt for all three of us, that was exquisite.

ROBERT SOUTHEY TO MISS BARKER.

KESWICK, April 3, 1804.

. . . Coleridge is gone for Malta, and his de-
parture affects me more than I let be seen.
Let what will trouble me, I bear a calm face;
and if the Boiling Well could be drawn (which,
however, it heaves and is agitated below, presents a smooth, undisturbed surface), that
should be my emblem. It is now almost ten
years since he and I first met, in my rooms at
Oxford, which meeting decided the destiny of
both; and now, when, after so many ups and
downs, I am, for a time, settled under his roof,
he is driven abroad in search of health. Ill he

is, certainly and sorely ill; yet I believe if his
mind was as well regulated as mine, the body
would be quite as manageable. I am perpetually pained and mortified by thinking what he
ought to be, for mine is an eye of microscopic
discernment to the faults of my friends; but
the tidings of his death would come upon me
more like a stroke of lightning than any evil I
have ever yet endured; almost it would make
me superstitious, for we were two ships that
left port in company. He has been sitting to
Northcote for Sir George Beaumont. There is
a finely painted, but dismal picture of him here,
with a companion of Wordsworth. I enjoy the
thought of your emotion when you will see
that portrait of Wordsworth. It looks as if he
had been a month in the condemned hole,
dieted upon bread and water, and debarred the
use of soap, water, razor, and combs; then
taken out of prison, placed in a cart, carried to
the usual place of execution, and had just suffered Jack Ketch to take off his cravat. The
best of this good joke is that the Wordsworths
are proud of the picture, and that his face is
the painter's ideal of excellence; and how the
devil the painter has contrived to make a like-

ness of so well-looking a man so ridiculously ugly *poozles* everybody. . . .

ROBERT SOUTHEY TO MISS MATILDA BETHAM.

KESWICK, July 2, 1808.

Your letter, my dear madam, has just prevented some arrangements which I was making for the conveyance of the picture to Cumberland. . . . We have heard of the miniature from a friend who saw it unexpectedly in the Exhibition, and was much struck with the likeness. I thank you likewise for your intentions with respect to Coleridge. You would have found him the most wonderful man living in conversation, but the most impracticable one for a painter, and had you begun the picture, it is ten thousand to one that you must have finished it from memory. His countenance is the most variable that I have ever seen; sometimes it is kindled with the brightest expression, and sometimes all its light goes out and is utterly extinguished. Nothing can convey stronger indications of power than his eye, eyebrow, and forehead; nothing can be more imbecile than all the rest of the face. Look at them separately, you would hardly think it possible that they could belong to one head; look at them to-gether, you wonder how they came so, and are puzzled what to expect from a character whose outward and visible signs are so contra-dictory. . . .

JOHN FOSTER TO MRS. BUNN.

BOURTON, January 28, 1815.

. . . I had no time . . . for any excursions for the mere purpose of looking about—except once so far beyond Bristol as St. Vincent's rocks, which, in an excessively cold and wet day, I contrasted with the magnificence of some of the scenes of North Wales. But even had there been higher rocks, and finer days, there was a circumstance capable of rendering them for a while matters of inferior interest. That circumstance was no other than my falling once more, after many years' interval, into the company of Coleridge, who was at the time lec-turing and talking in Bristol.

I could not conveniently hear more than one of his lectures (on Shakespeare), but it was a still higher luxury to hear him talk as much as would have been two or three lectures. I use

the word *luxury*, however, not without some
considerable qualification of its usual meaning,
since it may not seem exactly descriptive of a
thing involving much severe labor,—and this
one is forced often to undergo in the endeavor
to understand him, his thinking is of so sur-
passingly original and abstracted a kind. This
is the case often even in his recital of facts, as
that recital is continually mixed with some
subtle speculation. It was perfectly wonderful,
in looking back on a few hours of his conversation, to think what a quantity of perfectly
original speculation he had uttered, in language
incomparably rich in ornament and new combi-
nations. In point of theological opinion, he is
become, indeed, has now a number of years
been, it is said, highly orthodox. . . . His mind
contains an astonishing mass of knowledge,
while in his power and manner of putting it to
use, he displays more of what we mean by the
term genius than any mortal I ever saw or ever
expect to see. He is still living in a wandering,
precarious, and comfortless way, perpetually
forming projects which he has not the steady
resolution to prosecute long enough to accom-
plish. . . .

CHARLES LAMB TO WILLIAM WORDSWORTH.

LONDON, April 26, 1816.

. . . Coleridge is printing "Christabel," by
Lord Byron's recommendation to Murray, with
what he calls a vision, "Kubla Khan," which
said vision he repeats so enchantingly that it
irradiates and brings heaven and elysian bowers
into my parlor while he sings or says it; . . .
He is at present under the medical care of a
Mr. Gilman (Killman?) at Highgate, where he
plays at leaving off laud—m; I think his essen-
tials not touched; he is very bad, but then he
wonderfully picks up another day, and his face,
when he repeats his verses, hath its ancient
lory—an archangel a little damaged. . . .

SAMUEL TAYLOR COLERIDGE TO JOSIAH WEDGE-
WOOD.

KESWICK, September 16, 1803.

. . . William Hazlitt is a thinking, observant,
original man; of great power as a painter of
character-portraits, and far more in the manner
of the old painters than any living artist, but
the objects must be before him. He has no
imaginative memory; so much for his intellect-
uals. His manners are to ninety-nine in one-
hundred singularly repulsive; brow-hanging;

shoe-contemplating — strange. Sharp seemed
to like him, but Sharp saw him for only half an
hour, and that walking. He is, I verily believe,
kindly natured; is very fond of, attentive to,
and patient with children, but he is jealous,
gloomy, and of an irritable pride. With all
this there is much good in him. He is disinter-
ested; an enthusiastic lover of the great men
who have been before us. He says things that
are his own, in a way of his own; and though
from habitual shyness, and the outside of bear-
skin, at least of misanthropy, he is strangely
confused and dark in his conversation, and de-
livers himself of almost all his conceptions with
a *forceps*, yet he *says*, more than any man I ever
knew (you yourself only excepted), that which
is his own, in a way of his own; and ofttimes
when he has wearied his mind, and the juice
has come out and spread over his spirits, he
will gallop for half an hour together, with real
eloquence. He sends well-feathered thoughts
straight forward to the mark with a twang of
the bow-string. If you could recommend him
as a portrait painter, I should be glad. To be
your companion he is, in my opinion, utterly
unfit. His own health is fitful. . . .

CHARLES LAMB TO WILLIAM WORDSWORTH.

LONDON, June 26, 1805.

. . . W. Hazlitt is in town. I took him to see a very pretty girl, professedly, where there were two young girls—the very head and sum of the girlery was two young girls. They neither laughed, nor sneered, nor giggled, nor whispered; but they were young girls, and he sat and frowned blacker and blacker, indignant that there should be such a thing as youth and beauty, till he tore me away before supper in perfect misery, and owned he could not bear young girls; they drove him mad. So I took him home to my old nurse, where he recovered perfect tranquillity. Independent of this, and as I am not a young girl myself, he is a great acquisition to us. . . .

———

BENJAMIN ROBERT HAYDON TO DAVID WILKIE.

October 27, 1816.

I have been at Hampstead this fortnight for my eyes, and shall return with my body much stronger for application. The greater part of my time has been spent in Leigh Hunt's society, who is certainly one of the most delightful companions. Full of poetry and art and amiable humor, we argue always with full hearts on every thing but religion and Bonaparte, and we have resolved never to talk of these, particularly as I have been recently examining Voltaire's opinions concerning Christianity, and turmoiling my head to ascertain fully my right to put him into my picture!

Though Leigh Hunt is not deep in knowledge—moral, metaphysical, or classical,—yet he is intense in feeling, and has an intellect forever on the alert. He is like one of those instruments on three legs, which, throw it how you will, always pitches on two, and has a spike sticking forever up and ever ready for you. He "sets" at a subject with a scent like a pointer. He is a remarkable man, and created a sensation by his independence, his courage, his disinterestedness in public matters, and by the truth, acuteness, and taste of his dramatic criticisms he raised the rank of newspapers, and gave by his example a literary feeling to the weekly ones especially. . . . As a man, I know none with such an affectionate heart, if never opposed in his opinions. He has defects of course; one of his great defects is getting inferior people about him to listen, too fond of

Vol. I.

shining at any expense in society, and a love of approbation from the darling sex, bordering on weakness; though to women he is delightfully pleasant, yet they seem more to dawdle him as a delicate plant. I don't know if they do not put a confidence in him which to me would be mortifying.

He is a man of sensibility tinged with morbidity, and of such sensitive organization of body, that the plant is not more alive to touch than he. I remember once, walking in a field, we came to a muddy place concealed by grass. The moment Hunt touched it, he shrank back, saying, "It is muddy!" as if he meaned that it was full of adders. . . .

MRS. CAROLINE NORTON TO ABRAHAM HAYWARD.

May 8, 1856.

. . . If your article on Rogers was delayed a little, I really don't think it would be "a pity"; —if it comes out now, it will only be swallowed up in the shoal of reviews on "Table Talk," etc. A good thoughtful review a little while hence—a review of *Rogers*, not of "Table Talk," —will really be read and thought of, and will be curious, for I suppose no man ever was so

much attended to and thought of, who had so
slender a fortune and such calm abilities. I
am sure you will know what I mean: No man
ever *seemed* so important, who did so little, aye,
and said so little (in spite of table-talk), for his
fellow-men. His God was Harmony; and over
his life Harmony presided, sitting on a luke-
warm cloud. He was *not* the " poet, sage, and
philosopher " people expect to find he was, but
a man in whom the tastes (rare fact!) prepon-
derated over the passions; who defrayed the
expenses of his tastes as other men make out-
lay for the gratification of their passions; all
within limit of reason; he did not squander
more than won the affection of his seraglio, the
Nine Muses, nor bet upon Pegasus, though he
entered him for the races when he had a fair
chance of winning. He did nothing rash. I
am sure Rogers as a baby never fell down, *unless he was pushed;* but walked from chair to
chair of the drawing-room furniture steadily
and quietly till he reached the place where the
sunbeam fell on the carpet. He must always
have preferred a lullaby to the merriest game
of romps; and if he could have spoken would
have begged his long clothes might be made of

fine *Mull* muslin instead of cambric or jacquenet,
the first fabric being of incomparable softness,
and the two latter capable of that which he
loathed—*starch.*

He was the very embodiment of quiet, from
his voice to the last harmonious little picture
that hung in his lulled room, and a curious figure he seemed—an elegant, pale watch-tower,
showing forever what a quiet port literature
and the fine arts might offer, in an age of
"progress," when every one is tossing, struggling, wrecking, and foundering on a sea of
commercial speculation or political adventure ;
where people fight even over pictures, and if a
man does buy a picture, it is with the burning
desire to prove it is a Raphael to his yelping
enemies, rather than to point it out with a slow
white finger to his breakfasting friends. . . .

LADY DUFFERIN TO ABRAHAM HAYWARD.

DUFFERIN LODGE, HIGHGATE, February 8, 1858.

. . . My reminiscences of Rogers ? Yes, I
will endeavor to rub them up for your service.
To the best of my recollection, he was a fine,
robust-looking man, with a florid complexion
and something of a rollicking manner. The

heartiness and cordiality of his address had perhaps a tinge of rusticity, which, combined with
his peculiar costume (top-boots and cords), and
the unkempt luxuriance of his shaggy locks—
or am I thinking of the late archbishop of Can-
terbury? There is a slight confusion in my
ideas on this subject, so I had best go straight
to my less material souvenir of your old friend.

Jesting apart—I wish I could find any thing
either in my papers or my recollections to add
to your own interesting details about Rogers.
I am loth to say, now that he is gone (what I
often said in his lifetime), that I never could
lash myself into a feeling of affection or admiration for him. This may account for the paucity
of my stock of recollections respecting a really
remarkable man, to whom my grandfather had
obligations, and who always professed to feel a
great attachment to me and my family. To
tell the truth, there was a certain *unreality* in
him which repelled me. I have heard him say
many graceful things, but few kind ones, and
he never seemed to me thoroughly in earnest
save in expressing contempt or dislike. I have
always heard that he was very liberal in pecuniary matters — although the instances you

give (or rather, which your friend gives) do not
appear to merit the term generous. He gave
what he valued least—*money;* he never gave
what he valued most—admiration. It seemed
a positive pain to him to hear any modern poet
praised, and I remember his treating me with
rudeness almost bearish because I indiscreetly
avowed how much I admired Tennyson's " Prin-
cess." He was certainly witty ; it was wit in the
strictest estimation of the term ; the produce
of a keen and polished intellect sharpened by
long contact with the world and hardened by a
just confidence in his own powers ; but there
was little or no *humor* in him, nothing that
warmed or kindled fun or sympathy in others,
much that provoked retort.

The only " funny " thing I remember his saying was, on one occasion when we were accidentally left alone in the dark, after some jesting remark on the danger to my reputation—
"Ah ! my dear, if sweet 78 could come again !
Mais ces beaux jours sont passés." . . .

THOMAS CARLYLE TO RALPH WALDO EMERSON.

CHELSEA, August 5, 1844.

. . . Alfred is one of the few British or Foreign Figures (a not increasing number, I think !)

who are and remain beautiful to me—a true human soul, or some authentic approximation thereto, to whom your own soul can say, Brother. However, I doubt he will not come; he often skips me in these brief visits to town— skips everybody indeed, being a man solitary and sad, as certain men are, dwelling in an element of gloom—carrying a bit of Chaos with him, in short, which he is manufacturing into Cosmos!

Alfred is the son of a Lincolnshire Gentleman Farmer, I think; indeed, you see in his verses that he is a native of "moated granges," and green, fat pastures, not of mountains and their torrents and storms. He had his breeding at Cambridge, as if for the Law or Church; being master of a small annuity on his Father's decease, he preferred clubbing with his Mother and some Sisters, to live unpromoted and write Poems. In this way he lives still, now here, now there, the family always within reach of London, never in it, he himself making rare and brief visits, lodging in some old comrade's rooms. I think he must be under forty, not much under it." * One of the finest-looking

* He was born in 1809.

men in the world. A great shock of rusty-
dark hair, bright-laughing hazel eyes, massive
aquiline face, almost Indian-looking ; clothes
cynically loose, free-and-easy ; smokes infinite
tobacco. His voice is musical metallic, fit for
loud laughter and piercing wail, and all that
may lie between ; speech and speculation free
and plenteous. I do not meet, in these late
decades, such company over a pipe ! We shall
see what he will grow to. . . .

CHARLES LAMB TO MISS MARY DOROTHY WORDS-
WORTH.*

LONDON, June 14, 1805.

I have every reason to suppose that this illness, like all Mary's former ones, will be but
temporary. But I cannot always feel so. Meantime she is dead to me, and I miss a prop. All
my strength is gone, and I am like a fool,
bereft of her coöperation. I dare not think,
lest I should think wrong ; so used am I to
look up to her in the least and biggest perplex-

* Several of these letters are wholly autobiographical, and
a strict adherence to the plan of arrangement would have
placed them in the preceding section ; but it seemed best, at
some sacrifice of consistency, to bring together all the letters
relating to Charles and Mary Lamb.

ity. To say all that I know of her would be more than I think anybody could believe or understand; and when I hope to have her well again with me, it would be sinning against her feelings to go about to praise her; for I can conceal nothing that I do from her. She is older, and wiser, and better than I, and all my wretched imperfections I cover to myself by resolutely thinking on her goodness. She would share life and death, heaven and hell, with me. She lives but for me; and I know I have been wasting and teasing her life for five years past incessantly with my cursed ways of going on. But even in this upbraiding of myself, I am offending against her, for I know that she has cleaved to me for better, for worse; and if the balance has been against her hitherto, it was a noble trade. . . .

MISS MARY LAMB TO MISS SARAH STODDART.

May 14, 1806.

. . . Charles is very busy at the office; he will be kept there to-day till seven or eight o'clock, and he came home very *smoky and drinky* last night, so that I am afraid a hard day's work will not agree very well with him.

O dear! what shall I say next? Why, this I

will say next, that I wish you was with me ; I
have been eating a mutton chop all alone, and
I have been just looking in the pint porter-pot,
which I find quite empty, and yet I am still
very dry.   If you was with me, we would have
a glass of brandy and water ; but it is quite impossible to drink brandy and water by one's self ;
therefore, I must wait with patience till the
kettle boils. I hate to drink tea alone, it is worse
than dining alone.   We have got a fresh cargo
of biscuits from Captain Burney's.   I have——

Here I was interrupted, and a long, tedious
interval has intervened, during which I have
had neither time nor inclination to write a word.
The lodging *—that pride and pleasure of your
heart and mine—is given up, *and here he is
again*—Charles, I mean—as unsettled and as un-
determined as ever. When he went to the poor
lodging, after the holidays I told you he had
taken, he could not endure the solitariness of
them, and I had no rest for the sole of my foot
till I promised to believe his solemn protesta-
tions that he could and would write as well at
home as there.   Do you believe this?

  * Lamb had been trying the experiment of a den, away
from home.

I have no power over Charles—he will do what he will do. But I ought to have some little influence over myself. And therefore I am most manfully resolving to turn over a new leaf with my own mind. Your visit to us, though not a very comfortable one to yourself, has been of great use to me. I set you up in my fancy as a kind of *thing* that takes an interest in my concerns; and I hear you talking to me, and arguing the matter very learnedly when I gave way to despondency. You shall hear a good account of me and the progress I make in altering my fretful temper to a calm and quiet one. It is but being once thoroughly convinced one is wrong, to make one resolve to do so no more; and I know my dismal faces have been almost as great a drawback upon Charles's comfort as his feverish, teasing ways have been upon mine. Our love for each other has been the torment of our lives hitherto. I am most seriously intending to bend the whole force of my mind to counteract this, and I think I see some prospect of success.

Of Charles ever bringing any work to pass at home, I am very doubtful; and of the farce *

* " Mr. II."

succeeding, I have little or no hope ; but if I could once get into the way of being cheerful myself, I should see an easy remedy in leaving town and living cheaply, almost wholly alone ; but till I do find we really are comfortable alone, and by ourselves, it seems a dangerous experiment. We shall certainly stay where we are till after next Christmas ; and in the meantime, as I told you before, all my whole thoughts shall be to *change* myself into just such a cheerful soul as you would be in a lone house, with no companion but your brother. . . .

MISS MARY LAMB TO MISS SARAH STODDART.

June 2, 1806.

My " Tales " are to be published in separate story-books—I mean in single stories, like the children's little shilling books. I cannot send you them in Manuscript, because they are all in the Godwins's hands; but one will be published very soon, and then you shall have it *all in print*. I go on very well, and have no doubt but I shall always be able to hit upon some kind of a job to keep going on. . . .

Charles has written " Macbeth," " Othello," " King Lear," and has begun " Hamlet ";

you would like to see us, as we often sit writing
on one table (but not on one cushion sitting),
like Hermia and Helena in the " Midsummer
Night's Dream " ; or, rather, like an old literary
Darby and Joan, I taking snuff, and he groan-
ing all the while, and saying he can make
nothing of it, which he always says till he has
finished, and then he finds out he has made
something of it. . . .

MISS MARY LAMB TO MISS BARBARA BETHAM
(AGED 14).

November 2, 1814.

It is very long since I have met with such an
agreeable surprise as the sight of your letter, my
kind young friend, afforded me. Such a nice
letter as it is too ; and what a pretty hand you
write ! I congratulate you on this attainment
with great pleasure, because I have so often
felt the disadvantage of my wretched hand-
writing.

You wish for London news. I rely upon
your sister Ann for gratifying you in this respect, yet I have been endeavoring to recollect
who you might have seen here, and what may
have happened to them since ; and this effort
has only brought the image of little Barbara

Betham, unconnected with any other person, so strongly before my eyes, that I seem as if I had no other subject to write upon. Now, I think I see you with your feet propped upon the fender, your two hands spread out upon your knees—an attitude you always chose when we were in familiar confidential conversation together,—telling me long stories of your own home, where you now say you are " moping on with the same thing every day," and which then presented nothing but pleasant recollections to your mind. How well I remember your quiet steady face bent over your book! One day, conscience-stricken at having wasted so much of your precious time in reading, and feeling yourself, as you prettily said, " quite useless to me," you went to my drawers and hunted out some unhemmed pocket-handkerchiefs, and by no means could I prevail upon you to resume your story-books till you had hemmed them all. I remember, too, your teaching my little maid to read—your sitting with her a whole evening to console her for the death of her sister, and that she in her turn endeavored to become a comforter to you, the next evening, when you wept at the sight of

Mrs. Holcroft, from whose school you had recently eloped because you were not partial to sitting in the stocks. Those tears, and a few you once dropped when my brother teased you about your supposed fondness for an apple dumpling, were the only interruptions to the calm contentedness of your unclouded brow. We still remain the same as you left us, neither taller, nor wiser, nor perceptibly older; but three years must have made a great alteration in you. How very much, dear Barbara, I should like to see you!

We still live in Temple Lane, but I am now sitting in a room you never saw. Soon after you left us we were distressed by the cries of a cat, which seemed to proceed from the garrets adjoining ours, and only separated from ours by the locked door on the farther side of my brother's bedroom, which you know was the little room at the top of the kitchen stairs. We had the lock forced and let poor puss out from behind a panel of the wainscot, and she lived with us from that time, for we were in gratitude bound to keep her, as she had introduced us to four untenanted, unowned rooms, and by degrees we have taken possession of

these unclaimed apartments—first putting up
lines to dry our clothes, then moving my
brother's bed into one of these, more commodious than his own room.　And last winter, my
brother being unable to pursue a work he had
begun, owing to the kind interruptions of
friends who were more at leisure than himself,
I persuaded him that he might write at his
ease in one of these rooms, as he could not
then hear the door-knock, or hear himself denied to be at home, which was sure to make
him call out and convict the poor maid in a fib.
Here, I said, he might be almost really not at
home.　So I put in an old grate and made him
a fire in the largest of these garrets, and carried
in one table and one chair, and bid him write
away, and consider himself as much alone as if
he were in some lodging on the midst of Salis-
bury Plain, or any other wide unfrequented
place where he could expect few visitors to
break in upon his solitude.　I left him quite
delighted with his new acquisition ; but in a few
hours he came down again with a sadly dismal
face.　He could do nothing, he said, with those
bare whitewashed walls before his eyes.　He
could not write in that dull unfurnished prison.

The next day, beforè he came home from his office, I had gathered up various bits of old carpeting to cover the floor; and, to a little break the blank look of the bare walls, I hung up a few old prints that used to ornament the kitchen; and after dinner, with great boast of what an improvement I had made, I took Charles once more into his new study. A week of busy labors followed, in which I think you would not have disliked to have been our assistant. My brother and I almost covered the walls with prints, for which purpose he cut out every print from every book in his old library, coming in every now and then to ask my leave to strip a fresh poor author—which he might not do, you know, without my permission, as I am elder sister. There was such pasting, such consultation where their portraits, and where a series of pictures from Ovid, Milton, and Shakespeare would show to most advantage, and in what obscure corner authors of humbler note might be allowed to tell their stories. All the books gave up their stories but one—a translation from Ariosto—a delicious set of four-and-twenty prints, and for which I had marked out a conspicuous place;

Vol. I.

when lo ! we found at the moment the scissors were going to work that a part of the poem was printed at the back of every picture.   What a cruel disappointment !   To conclude this long story about nothing, the poor, despised garret is now called the print room, and is become our most favorite sitting-room. . . . The lions still live in Exeter Change.   Returning home through the Strand, I often hear them roar about twelve o'clock at night.   I never hear them without thinking of you, because you seemed so pleased with the sight of them, and said your young companions would stare when you told them you had seen a lion.   And now, my dear Barbara, farewell ; I have not written such a long letter a long time, but I am very sorry I had nothing amusing to write about. . . .

CHARLES LAMB TO MISS HUTCHINSON.

London, October 19, 1815.

I am forced to be the replier to your letter, for Mary has been ill, and gone from home these five weeks yesterday. . . . I don't know but the recurrence of these illnesses might help me to sustain her death better than if we had had no partial separations.   But I won't talk of

death. I will imagine us immortal, or forget
that we are otherwise. By God's blessing, in
a few weeks we may be making our meal together, or sitting in the front row of the pit at
Drury Lane, or taking our evening walk past
the theatres, to look at the outside of them, at
least, if not to be tempted in. Then we forget
we are assailable; we are strong for the time as
rocks,—"the wind is tempered to the shorn
Lambs." . . .

CHARLES LAMB TO WILLIAM WORDSWORTH.

1815.

. . . I wish you would write more criticism
about Spenser, etc. I think I could say something about him myself, but, Lord bless me!
these "merchants and their spicy drugs," which
are so harmonious to sing of, they lime-twig up
my poor soul and body, till I shall forget I ever
thought myself a bit of a genius! I can't even
put a few thoughts on paper for a newspaper.
I engross when I should pen a paragraph.
Confusion blast all mercantile transactions, all
traffic, exchange of commodities, intercourse
between nations, all the consequent civilization and wealth, and amity, and link of society,

and getting rid of prejudices, and getting a knowledge of the face of the globe; and rot the very firs of the forest that look so romantic alive, and die into desks! *Vale.*

CHARLES LAMB TO MISS MATILDA BETHAM.

LONDON, June 1, 1816.

All this while I have been tormenting myself with the thought of having been ungracious to you, and you have been all the while accusing yourself. Let us absolve one another, and be quiet. My head is in such a state from incapacity for business that I certainly know it to be my duty not to undertake the veriest trifle in addition. I hardly know how I can go on. I have tried to get some redress by explaining my health, but with no great success. No one can tell how ill I am because it does not come out to the exterior of my face, but lies in my skull deep and invisible. I wish I was leprous, and black jaundiced skin-over, and that all was as well within as my cursed looks. You must not think me worse than I am. I am determined not to be over-set, but to give up business rather, and get 'em to allow me a trifle for services past. O that I had been a shoemaker

or a baker, or a man of large independent fortune! O darling laziness! heaven of Epicurus!
Saint's Everlasting Rest! that I could drink
vast potations of thee thro' all unmeasured eternity—Otium *cum* vel *sine* dignitate. Scandalous, dishonorable, any kind of *repose*. I stand
not upon the *dignified sort*. Accursed, damned
desks, commerce, business. Inventions of that
old original busybody, brain-working Satan—
Sabbathless, restless Satan. A curse relieves;
do you ever try it? . . .

CHARLES LAMB TO BERNARD BARTON.

March 23, 1825.

I have had no impulse to write, or attend to
any single object but myself for weeks past—
my single self, I by myself—I. I am sick of
hope deferred. The grand wheel is in agita-
tion, that is to turn up my fortune; but round
it rolls, and will turn up nothing. I have a
glimpse of freedom, of becoming a gentleman
at large; but I am put off from day to day.
I have offered my resignation, and it is neither
accepted nor rejected. Eight weeks am I kept
in this fearful suspense. Guess what an absorb-
ing stake I feel it. I am not conscious of the

existence of friends present or absent. The
East India Directors alone can be that thing to
me or not. I have just learned that nothing
will be decided this week. Why the next?
Why any week? It has fretted me into an itch
of the fingers; I rub 'em against paper, and
write to you, rather than not allay this scor-
buta. . . .

———

CHARLES LAMB TO WILLIAM WORDSWORTH.

COLEBROOK COTTAGE, April 6, 1825.

I have been several times meditating a letter
to you concerning the good thing which has
befallen me; but the thought of poor Monkhouse came across me. He was one that I had
exulted in the prospect of congratulating me.
He and you were to have been the first partici-
pators; for indeed it has been ten weeks since
the first motion of it. Here am I then, after
thirty-three years' slavery, sitting in my own
room at eleven o'clock this finest of all April
mornings, a freed man, with £441 a year for
the remainder of my life, live I as long as John
Dennis, who outlived his annuity and starved
at ninety: £441, *i. e.*, £450, with a deduction
of £9 for a provision secured to my sister, she

being survivor, the pension guaranteed by Act Georgii Tertii, etc.

I came home FOR EVER on Tuesday in last week. The incomprehensibleness of my condition overwhelmed me. It was like passing from life into eternity. Every year to be as long as three, *i. e.*, to have three times as much real time—time that is my own, in it! I wandered about thinking I was happy, but feeling I was not. But that tumultuousness is passing off, and I begin to understand the nature of the gift. Holydays, even the annual month, were always uneasy joys—their conscious fugitiveness;—the craving after making the most of them. Now, when all is holyday, there are no holydays. I can sit at home, in rain or shine, without a restless impulse for walkings. I am daily steadying, and shall soon find it as natural to me to be my own master, as it has been irksome to have had a master. Mary wakes every morning with an obscure feeling that some good has happened to us. . . .

CHARLES LAMB TO BERNARD BARTON.
April 6, 1825.

My spirits are so tumultuary with the novelty of my recent emancipation, that I have scarce steadiness of hand, much more mind, to compose a letter. I am free, B. B.—free as air!

> " The little bird that wings the sky
> Knows no such liberty."

I was set free on Tuesday in last week at four o'clock. I came home for ever!

I have been describing my feelings as well as I can to Wordsworth in a long letter, and don't care to repeat. Take it briefly, that for a few days I was painfully oppressed by so mighty a change; but it is becoming daily more natural to me. I went and sat among 'em all at my old thirty-three-years' desk yester morning; and, deuce take me, if I had not yearnings at leaving all my old pen-and-ink fellows, merry, sociable lads—at leaving them in the lurch, fag, fag, fag! The comparison of my own superior felicity gave me any thing but pleasure. . . .

CHARLES LAMB TO WILLIAM WORDSWORTH.

May, 1825.

I write post-haste to ensure a frank. Thanks for your hearty congratulations! I may now date from the sixth week of my " Hegira, or Flight from Leadenhall." I have lived so much in it, that a summer seems already past; and

't is but early May yet with you and other people. How I look down on the slaves and
drudges of the world! Its inhabitants are a
vast cotton-web of spin-spin-spinners! O the
carking cares! O the money-grubbers! Sempi-
ternal muckworms!

Some d—d people are come in, and I
must finish abruptly. By d—d I only mean
deuced. . . .

CHARLES AND MARY LAMB TO MR. AND MRS. ED-
WARD MOXON.*

EDMONTON, August, 1833.

Dear Mr. and Mrs. Moxon :—Time very short.
I wrote to Miss Fryer, and had the sweetest
letter about you, Emma, that ever friendship
dictated. "I am full of good wishes, I am
crying with good wishes," she says; but you
shall see it. . . . I am calm, sober, happy. Turn
over for the reason. I got home from Dover
Street, by 'eavens, *half as sober as a judge*. I am
turning over a new leaf, as I hope you will now—

[The turn of the leaf presented the following from Mary
Lamb :]

* Miss Emma Islola, one of the Lambs' dearest friends, had
just been married to Mr. Edward Moxon. At the time of the
wedding, Mary Lamb was suffering one of the worst of her
illnesses.

My Dear Emma and Edward Moxon—Accept my sincere congratulations, and imagine more good wishes than my weak nerves will let me put into good set words. The dreary blank of *unanswered questions* which I ventured to ask in vain was cleared up on the wedding-day by Mrs. W. taking a glass of wine, and, with a total change of countenance, begging leave to drink Mr. and Mrs. Moxon's health. It restored me from that moment, as if by an electrical stroke, to the entire possession of my senses. I never felt so calm and quiet after a similar illness as I do now. I feel as if all tears were wiped from my eyes, and all care from my heart.

[At the foot of the letter is the following by Charles :]

Dears, again :—Your letter interrupted a seventh game at picquet which *we* were having, after walking to Wright's and purchasing shoes. We pass our time in cards, walks, and reading. We attack Tasso soon.

C. L.

Never was such a calm or such a recovery. 'T is her own words, undictated.

BENJAMIN ROBERT HAYDON TO WILLIAM WORDS-
WORTH.

LONDON, October 16, 1842.

In the words of our dear departed friend,
Charles Lamb, " You good-for-nothing old
Lake-poet," what has become of you? Do
you remember his saying that at my table in
1819, with " Jerusalem " towering behind us in
the painting room, and Keats and your friend
Monkhouse of the party? Do you remember
Lamb voting me absent, and then making a
speech descanting on my excellent port, and
proposing a vote of thanks? Do you remember his then voting me present—I had never
left my chair—and informing me of what had
been done during my retirement, and hoping I
was duly sensible of the honor? Do you remember the Commissioner (of Stamps and
Taxes) who asked you if you did not think
Milton a great genius, and Lamb getting up
and asking leave with a candle to examine his
phrenological development? Do you remember poor dear Lamb, whenever the Commissioner was equally profound, saying: " My son
John went to bed with his breeches on," to the
dismay of the learned man? Do you remem-

ber you and I and Monkhouse getting Lamb
out of the room by force, and putting on his
great-coat, he reiterating his earnest desire to
examine the Commissioner's skull? And don't
you remember Keats proposing "Confusion to
the Memory of Newton," and upon your insist-
ing upon an explanation before you drank it, his
saying: "Because he destroyed the poetry of
the rainbow by reducing it to a prism." Ah!
my dear old friend, you and I shall never see
such days again! The peaches are not so big
now as they were in our days. . . .

<hr>

DANIEL MACMILLAN TO DAVID WATT.

LONDON, September 29, 1842.

. . . Hare * spoke in the most affectionate
manner of Charles Lamb. He dined with him
and a large party of literati once. De Quincey
was there. I daresay you know that De Q. is
a very little man. Hare was sitting next to
Lamb; De Q. was on the opposite side of the
table. Lamb touched Hare, and said, quite
loud, so that the whole table might hear him:
"Do you see that little man?" (pointing to De
Q.) "Well, though he is so little, he has written

* Archdeacon Julius Hare.

a thing about Macbeth better than any thing I could write;—no—not better than any thing I could write, but I could not write any thing better." Immediately afterwards he said to Hare: "I am a very foolish fellow. For instance, I have taken a fancy for you. I wish you would come and sup with me to-morrow night. I will give you crab—perhaps lobster." . . .

MISS HANNAH MORE TO ——

LONDON, 1776.

I dined in the Adelphi yesterday. It was a particular occasion—an annual meeting, where nothing but men are usually asked. I was, however, of the party, and an agreeable day it was to me. I have seldom heard so much wit, under the banner of so much decorum. I mention this, because I was told it was a day of license, and that everybody was to say what they pleased. Coleman and Dr. Schomberg were of the party; the rest were chiefly old doctors of divinity. I had a private whisper that I must dine there again to-day, to assist at the celebration of the birthday. We had a little snug dinner in the library. At six, I begged leave to come home, as I expected my *petite*

assemblée a little after seven. Mrs. Garrick offered me all her fine things, but, as I hate admix-
tures of finery and meanness, I refused every
thing except a little cream and a few sorts of
cake. They came at seven. The *dramatis per-
sonæ* were Mrs. Boscawen, Mrs. Garrick, and Miss
Reynolds; my beaux were Dr. Johnson, Dean
Tucker, and last, but not least in our love, David Garrick. You know that wherever Johnson
is, the confinement to the tea-table is rather a
durable situation; and it was an hour and a
half before I got my enlargement. However,
my ears were opened, though my tongue was
locked, and they all staid till near eleven.

Garrick was the very soul of the company,
and I never saw Johnson in such perfect humor. Sally knows we have often heard that one
can never properly enjoy the company of these
two unless they are together. There is great
truth in this remark; for after the Dean and
Mrs. Boscawen (who were the only strangers)
were withdrawn, and the rest stood up to go,
Johnson and Garrick began a close encounter
telling old stories, "e'en from their boyish
days" at Lichfield. We all stood round them
above an hour, laughing, in defiance of every

rule of decorum and Chesterfield. I believe we
should not have thought of sitting down or
of parting, had not an impertinent watchman
been saucily vociferous. Johnson outstaid them
all, and sat with me half an hour.

I'll tell you the most ridiculous circumstance
in the world. After dinner Garrick took up the
Monthly Review (civil gentlemen, by-the-by,
these Monthly Reviewers), and read " Sir El-
dred " * with all his pathos and all his graces. I
think I was never so ashamed in my life ; but
he read it so superlatively, that I cried like
a child. Only think what a scandalous thing,
to cry at the reading of one's own poetry ! I
could have beaten myself ; for it looked as if I
thought it very moving, which, I can truly say,
is far from being the case. But the beauty of
the jest lies in this : Mrs. Garrick twinkled as
well as I, and made as many apologies for crying at her husband's reading, as I did for crying
at my own verses. She got out of the scrape
by pretending she was touched at the story,
and I by saying the same of the reading. It
furnished us with a great laugh at the catastro-
phe, when it would really have been decent to
have been a little sorrowful.

* A poem by Miss More.

MISS FRANCES BURNEY TO SAMUEL CRISP.

June, 1782.

At the Knight of Plympton's* house, on Richmond Hill, next to the Star and Garter, we were met by the Bishop of St. Asaph, who stands as high in general esteem for agreeability as for worth and learning; and by his accomplished and spirited daughter, Miss Shipley. My father was already acquainted with both; and to both I was introduced by Miss Palmer.

No other company was mentioned; but some smiling whispers passed between Sir Joshua, Miss Palmer, and my father, that awakened in me a notion that the party was not yet complete; and with that notion, an idea that Mr. Burke might be the awaited chief of the assemblage; for, as they knew I had long had as much eagerness to see Mr. Burke, as I had fears of meeting his expectations, I thought they might forbear naming him, to save me a fit of fright.

Sir Joshua, who, though full of kindness, dearly loves a little innocent malice, drew me soon afterwards to a window to look at the beautiful prospect below—the soft meandering

* Sir Joshua Reynolds.

of the Thames, and the brightly picturesque situation of the elegant white house which Horace Walpole had made the habitation of Lady Diana Beauclerk and her fair progeny,— in order to gather, as he afterwards laughingly acknowledged, my sentiments of the view, that he might compare them with those of Mr. Burke on the same scene. However, I escaped, luckily, falling, through ignorance, into such a competition, by the entrance of a large, though unannounced, party in mass. For, as this was only a visit of a day, there were very few servants; and those few, I suppose, were preparing the dinner apartment, for this group appeared to have found its own way up to the drawing-room with an easiness as well suited to its humor, by the gay air of its approach, as to that of Sir Joshua, who holds ceremony almost in horror, and who received them without any form or apology.

He quitted me, however, to go forward and greet with distinction a lady who was in the set. They were all familiarly recognized by the Bishop and Miss Shipley, as well as by Miss Palmer; and some of them by my father, whose own face wore an expression of pleasure,

Vol. I.

that helped to fix a conjecture in my mind that one among them, whom I peculiarly signalized, tall, and of fine deportment, with an air of courtesy and command, might be Edmund Burke.

Excited as I felt by this idea, I continued at my picturesque window, as all the company were strangers to me, till Miss Palmer gave her hand to the tall, suspected, but unknown personage, saying, in a half whisper: "Have I kept my promise at last?" and then, but in a lower tone still, and pointing to the window, she pronounced "Miss Burney."

As this seemed intended for private information, previously to an introduction, be the person whom he might, though accidentally it was overheard, I instantly bent my head out of the window, as if not attending to them. Yet I caught, unavoidably, the answer, which was uttered in a voice most emphatic, though low:—"Why did you tell me it was Miss Burney? Did you think I should not have known it?"

An awkward feeling now, from having still no certainty of my surmise, or of what it might produce, made me seize a spy-glass and set about re-examining the prospect, till a pat on my arm soon after, by Miss Palmer, turned me

round to the company, just as the still unknown, to my great regret, was going out of
the room with a footman, who seemed to call
him away upon some sudden summons of business. But my father, who was at Miss Palmer's
elbow, said · "Fanny, Mr. Gibbon!" This,
too, was a great name ; but of how different
a figure and presentation! Fat and ill-con-
structed, Mr. Gibbon has cheeks of such prodigious chubbiness that they envelop his nose
so completely as to render it, in profile, absolutely invisible. His look and manner are
placidly mild, but rather effeminate ; his voice
—for he was speaking to Sir Joshua at a little
distance—is gentle, but of studied precision of
accent. Yet, with these Brobdignatious cheeks,
his neat little feet are of a miniature description ; and with these, as soon as I turned round,
he hastily described a quaint sort of circle, with
small quick steps, and a dapper gait, as if to
mark the alacrity of his approach, and then
stopping short, when full face to me, he made
so singularly profound a bow that—though
hardly able to keep my gravity—I felt myself
blush deeply at its undue, but palpably intended, obsequiousness.

This demonstration, however, over, his sense of politeness, or project of flattery, was satisfied; for he spoke not a word, though his gallant advance seemed to indicate a design of bestowing upon me a little rhetorical touch of a compliment. But, as all eyes in the room were suddenly cast upon us both, it is possible he partook a little himself of the embarrassment he could not but see that he occasioned; and was, therefore, unwilling, or unprepared, to hold forth so publicly upon—he scarcely, perhaps, knew what! for, unless my partial Sir Joshua should just then have poured it into his ears, how little is it likely Mr. Gibbon should have heard of " Evelina!"

But at this moment, to my great relief, the unknown again appeared; and with a spirit, an air, a deportment that seemed to spread around him the glow of pleasure with which he himself was visibly exhilarated. But speech was there none, for dinner, which I suppose had awaited him, was at the same instant proclaimed; and all the company, in a mixed, quite irregular, and even confused manner, descended, *sans ceremonie*, to the eating parlor.

The unknown, however, catching the arm
and the trumpet of Sir Joshua, as they were
coming down stairs, murmured something in
a rather reproachful tone in the knight's ear;
to which Sir Joshua made no audible answer.
But when he had placed himself at his table, he
called out smilingly, "Come, Miss Burney, will
you take a seat next mine?" adding, as if to
reward my very alert compliance, "and then,
Mr. Burke shall sit on your other side!"

"O no, indeed!" cried the sprightly Miss
Shipley, who was also next to Sir Joshua; "I
sha'n't agree to that. Mr. Burke must sit next
to me; I won't consent to part with him. So
pray come, and sit down quiet, Mr. Burke."

Mr. Burke—for Mr. Burke, Edmund Burke
it was—smiled and obeyed.

"I only proposed it to make my peace with
Mr. Burke," said Sir Joshua, passively, "by
giving him that place, for he has been scolding
me all the way down stairs for not having introduced him to Miss Burney; however, I must
do it now. Mr. Burke—Miss Burney!"

We both half rose to reciprocate a little salu-
tation, and Mr. Burke said: "I have been com-
plaining to Sir Joshua that he left me wholly

to my own sagacity, which, however, did not here deceive me!"

Delightedly as my dear father, who had never before seen Mr. Burke in private, enjoyed this encounter, I, my dear Mr. Crisp, had a delight in it that transcended all comparison. No expectation that I had formed of Mr. Burke, either from his works, his speeches, his character, or his fame, had anticipated to me such a man as I now met. He appeared, perhaps, at this moment, to the highest possible advantage, in health, vivacity and spirits. Removed from the perpetual aggravations of party contentions that at times, by inflaming his passions, seem, momentarily at least, to disorder his character, he was lulled into gentleness by the grateful feelings of prosperity. . . . He looked, indeed, as if he had no wish but to diffuse philanthropy, pleasure, and genial gayety all around.

His figure, when he is not negligent in his carriage, is noble, his air commanding, his address graceful; his voice clear, penetrating, sonorous, and powerful; his language copious, eloquent, and changefully impressive; his manners are attractive; his conversation is past all praise! . . . How proud should I be to give you a sample of the conversation of Mr. Burke! But the subjects were in general so fleeting, his ideas so full of variety, of gayety, and of matter; and he darted from one of them to another with such rapidity, that the manner, the eye, the air, with which all was pronounced, ought to be separately delineated, to do any justice to the effect that every sentence, nay, that every word, produced upon his admiring hearers and beholders.

THOMAS CARLYLE TO HIS WIFE.

LONDON, August 17, 1831.

I left off on the eve of seeing Irving and taking tea with Godwin. The first object I accomplished. Irving, with his huge fleece of now grizzled hair, was eager to talk with me and see me often.

Next came Godwin. Did you not grudge me that pleasure, now? At least, mourn that you were not there with me! Grudge not, mourn not, dearest Jeannie; it was the most unutterable stupidity ever enacted on this earth. We went, Jack and I, to the huge Frenchwoman, Mrs. Kenny's (once Mrs. Holcroft), Badams' mother-in-law, a sort of more masculine

Aurelia (" Wilhelm Meister "), who lives, moves, and has her being among plays, operas, dilettantes, and playwrights. Badams and his wife had not returned from the country, but in a few minutes came. Mrs. Godwin already sat gossiping in the dusk—an old woman of no significance ; by-and-by dropped in various playwrightesses and playwrights, whom I did not even look at ; shortly before candles Godwin himself (who had been drinking *good* green tea by his own hearth before stirring out). He is a bald, bushy-browed, thick, hoary, hale little figure, taciturn enough, and speaking, when he does speak, with a certain *epigrammatic* spirit, wherein, except a little shrewdness, there is nothing but the most commonplace character. (I should have added that he wears spectacles, has full gray eyes, a very large, blunt, characterless nose, and ditto chin). By degrees I hitched myself near him, and was beginning to open him and to open on him, for he had stared twice at me, when suddenly enough began a speaking of French among the Kennys and Badamsinas (for they are all French-English), and presently Godwin was summoned off to— take a hand at whist ! *I* had already flatly declined. There did the philosopher sit, and a swarm of noisy children, chattering women, noisy dilettantes round him; and two women literally crashing hoarse thunder out of a piano (for it was louder than an iron forge) under pretext of its being music by Rossini. I thought of my own piano, and the far different fingering it got; looked sometimes not without sorrow at the long-nosed whist-player, and in the space of an hour (seeing supper about to be laid in another room) took myself away.

THOMAS BABINGTON MACAULAY TO MISS HANNAH MORE MACAULAY.

LONDON, July 25, 1831.

On Saturday evening I went to Holland House. . . . Her Ladyship, for an *esprit fort*, is the greatest coward I ever saw. The last time I was there she was frightened out of her wits by the thunder. She closed all the shutters, drew all the curtains, and ordered candles in broad day to keep out the lightning, or rather the appearance of the lightning. On Saturday she was in a terrible taking about the cholera; talked of nothing else; refused to eat any ice because somebody said that ice was

bad for the cholera, was sure that the cholera
was at Glasgow; and asked me why a cordon
of troops was not instantly placed around that
town to prevent all intercourse between the in-
fected and the healthy spots.   Lord Holland
made light of her fears.   He is a thoroughly
good-natured, open, sensible man ; very lively ;
very intellectual ; well read in politics, and in the
lighter literature both of ancient and modern
times.   He sets me more at ease than almost
any person that I know, by a certain good-
humored way of contradicting that he has.   He
always begins by drawing down his shaggy
eyebrows, making a face extremely like his
uncle, wagging his head, and saying : " Now do
you know, Mr. Macaulay, I do not quite see
that.   How do you make that out ?"   He tells
a story delightfully, and bears the pain of his
gout and the confinement and privations to
which it subjects him, with admirable fortitude
and cheerfulness.   Her Ladyship is all courtesy
and kindness to me ; but her demeanor to some
others, particularly to poor Allen, is such as it
quite pains me to witness.   He is really treated
like a negro slave.   " Mr. Allen, go into my
drawing-room and bring my reticule."   " Mr.

Allen, go and see what can be the matter that they do not bring up the dinner." "Mr. Allen, there is not enough turtle-soup for you. You must take gravy-soup or none." . . .

———

THOMAS CARLYLE TO HIS BROTHER.

CHELSEA, March 17, 1840.

. . . At the dear cost of a shattered set of nerves and head set whirling for the next eight-and-forty hours, I did see lords and lions— Lord Holland and Lady, Lord Normanby, etc. —and then, for *soirée* up-stairs, Morpeth, Lansdowne, French Guizot, the Queen of Beauty,* etc. Nay, Pickwick, too, was of the same dinner-party, though they do not seem to heed him overmuch. He is a fine little fellow—Boz, I think. Clear blue, intelligent eyes, eyebrows that he arches amazingly, large, protrusive, rather loose mouth, a face of most extreme *mobility*, which he shuttles about—eyebrows, eyes, mouth and all—in a very singular manner while speaking. Surmount this with a loose coil of common-colored hair, and set it on a small compact figure, very small, and dressed à la D'Orsay rather than well—this is Pickwick.

* Lady Blessington.

For the rest, a quiet, shrewd-looking, little fellow, who seems to guess pretty well what he is and what others are. Lady Holland is a brown-skinned, silent, sad, concentrated, proud old dame. Her face, when you see it in profile, has something of the falcon character, if a falcon's bill was straight ; and you see much of the white of her eye. Notable word she spake none—sate like one wont to be obeyed and entertained. Old Holland, whose legs are said to be almost turned to *stone*, pleased me much. A very large, bald head, small, gray, invincible, composed-looking eyes, the immense tuft of an eyebrow which all the Foxes have, stiff upper lip, roomy mouth and chin, short, angry, yet modest nose. I saw there a fine old *Jarl*—an honest, obstinate, candid, wholesomely limited, very effectual and estimable old man. Of the rest I will not say a syllable, not even of the Queen of Beauty, who looked rather withered and unwell.

MRS. THOMAS CARLYLE TO HER HUSBAND.

CHELSEA, September 23, 1845.

" Nothink " for you to-day in the shape of inclosure, unless I inclose a letter from Mrs. Paulet to myself, which you will find as " entertain-

ing" to the full as any of mine. And *nothink*
to be told either, except all about the play,*
and upon my honor, I do not feel as if I had
penny-a-liner genius enough, this cold morning,
to make much entertainment out of that.
Enough to clasp one's hand, and exclaim, like
Helen before the Virgin and Child, "Oh, how
expensive!" But "how did the creatures get
through it?" Too well; and not well enough!
The public theatre, scenes painted by Stans-
field, costumes "rather exquisite," together with
the certain amount of proficiency in the ama-
teurs, overlaid all idea of private theatricals;
and, considering it as public theatricals, the
acting was "most insipid," not one performer
among them that could be called good, and
none that could be called absolutely bad.
Douglas Jerrold seemed to me the best, the
oddity of his appearance greatly helping him;
he played *Stephen the Cull.* Forster as *Kitely*
and Dickens as *Captain Bobadil* were much on
a par; But Forster preserved his identity, even
through his loftiest flights of Macreadyism;
while poor little Dickens, all painted in black

* Private theatricals got up by Dickens and Forster for some
benevolent purpose.—J. A. FROUDE.

and red, and affecting the voice of a man of six feet, would have been unrecognizable for the mother that bore him! On the whole, to get up the smallest interest in the thing, one needed to be always reminding one's self: "all these actors were once men!" and will be men again to-morrow morning. The greatest wonder for me was how they had contrived to get together some six or seven hundred ladies and gentlemen (judging from the clothes) at this season of the year; and all utterly unknown to me, except some half-dozen.

So long as I kept my seat in the dress circle I recognized only Mrs. Macready (in one of the four private boxes), and in my nearer neighborhood Sir Alexander and Lady Gordon. But in the interval betwixt the play and the farce, I took a notion to make my way to Mrs. Macready. John, of course, declared the thing "clearly impossible, no use trying it"; but a servant of the theatre, overhearing our debate, politely offered to escort me where I wished; and then John, having no longer any difficulties to surmount, followed, to have his share in what advantages might accrue from the change. Passing through a long dim passage, I came on a tall man leant to the wall, with his head touching the ceiling like a caryatid, to all appearance asleep, or resolutely trying it under most unfavorable circumstances. "Alfred Tennyson!" I exclaimed, in joyful surprise. "Well!" said he, taking the hand I held out to him, and forgetting to let it go again. "I did not know you were in town," said I. "I should like to know who you are," said he; "I know that I know you, but I cannot tell your name." And I had actually to name myself to him. Then he woke up in good earnest, and said he had been meaning to come to Chelsea. "But Carlyle is in Scotland," I told him with due humility. "So I heard from Spedding already, but I asked Spedding, would he go with me to see Mrs. Carlyle? and he said he would." I told him if he really meant to come, he had better not wait for backing, under the present circumstances; and then pursued my way to the Macreadys' box; where I was received by William (whom I had not divined) with a "Gracious heavens!" and spontaneous dramatic start, which made me all but answer, "Gracious heavens!" and start dramatically in my turn. And then I was kissed all round by his women;

and poor Nell Gwyn, Mrs. M—— G——, seemed almost pushed by the general enthusiasm on the distracted idea of kissing me also! They would not let me return to my stupid place, but put in a third chair for me in front of their box; " and the latter end of that woman was better than the beginning." . . .

THE FAMILY.

***

LORD CUTHBERT COLLINGWOOD TO HIS WIFE.

OCEAN, June 16, 1806.

This day, my love, is the anniversary of our marriage, and I wish you many happy returns of it. If ever we have peace, I hope to spend my latter days amid my family, which is the only sort of happiness I can enjoy. After this life of labor, to retire to peace and quietness is all I look for in the world. Should we decide to change the place of our dwelling, our route would of course be to the southward of Morpeth; but then I should be forever regretting those beautiful views which are nowhere to be exceeded; and even the rattling of that old wagon that used to pass our door at six o'clock on a winter's morning had its charms. The fact is, whenever I think how I am to be happy again, my thoughts carry me back to Morpeth, where, out of the fuss and parade of the world,

surrounded by those I loved most dearly, and
who loved me, I enjoyed as much happiness as
my nature is capable of. Many things that I
see in the world give me a distaste to the finery
of it. The great knaves are not like those poor
unfortunates, who, driven perhaps to distress
from accidents which they could not prevent,
or at least not educated in principles of honor
and honesty, are hanged for some little thiev-
ery; while a knave of education and high-
breeding, who brandishes his honor in the eyes
of the world, would rob a state to its ruin.
For the first, I feel pity and compassion; for
the latter, abhorrence and contempt: they are
the tenfold vicious.

Have you read—but what I am more interested about, is your sister with you, and is she
well and happy? Tell her—God bless her!—
I wish I were with you, that we might have a
good laugh. God bless me! I have scarcely
laughed these three years. I am here with a
very reduced force, having been obliged to
make detachments to all quarters. This leaves
me weak, while the Spaniards and French
within are daily gaining strength. They have
patched and pieced until they have now a very

considerable fleet. Whether they will venture out I do not know; if they come, I have no doubt we shall do an excellent deed, and then I will bring them to England myself.

How do the dear girls go on? I would have them taught geometry, which is, of all sciences in the world, the most entertaining; it expands the mind more to the knowledge of all things in nature, and better teaches to distinguish between truths and such things as have the appearance of being truths, yet are not, than any other. . . .

Tell me, how do the trees which I planted, thrive? Is there shade under the three oaks for a comfortable summer-seat? Do the poplars grow at the walk, and does the wall of the terrace stand firm? My bankers tell me that all my money in their hands is exhausted by fees on the peerage, and that I am in their debt, which is a new epoch in my life, for it is the first time I was ever in debt since I was a midshipman. Here I get nothing; but then my expenses are nothing, and I do not want it particularly, now that I have got my knives, forks, tea-pot, and the things you were so kind as to send me.

SIR RICHARD STEELE TO HIS WIFE.

June 20, 1717.

DEAR PRUE:—I have yours of the 14th, and am infinitely obliged to you for the length of it. I do not know another whom I could commend for that circumstance; but where we entirely love, the continuance of any thing they do to please us is a pleasure. As for your relations; once for all, pray take it for granted that my regard and conduct towards all and singular of them shall be as you direct.

I hope, by the grace of God, to continue what you wish me, every way an honest man. My wife and my children are the objects that have wholly taken up my heart; and as I am not invited or encouraged in any thing which regards the public, I am easy under that neglect or envy of my past actions, and cheerfully contract that diffusive spirit within the interests of my own family. You are the head of us; and I stoop to a female reign, as being naturally made the slave of beauty. But, to prepare for our manner of living when we are again together, give me leave to say, while I am here at leisure, and come to lie at Chelsea, what I think may contribute to our better way of liv-

ing. I very much approve Mrs. Evans and her
husband, and, if you take my advice, I would
have them have a being in our house, and Mrs.
Clark the care and inspection of the nursery. I
would have you entirely at leisure, to pass your
time with me, in diversions, in books, in enter-
tainments, and no manner of business intrude
upon us but at stated times: for, though you
are made to be the delight of my eyes, and
food of all my senses and faculties, yet a turn
of care and housewifery, and I know not what
prepossession against conversation-pleasures,
robs me of the witty and the handsome woman,
to a degree not to be expressed. I will work
my brains and fingers to procure us plenty of
things, and demand nothing of you but to take
delight in agreeable dresses, cheerful discourses,
and gay sights, attended by me. This may be
done by putting the kitchen and the nursery in
the hands I propose ; and I shall have nothing
to do but to pass as much time at home as I
possibly can in the best company in the world.
We cannot tell here what to think of the trial
of my Lord Oxford; if the Ministry are in
earnest in that, and I should see it will be extended to a length of time, I will leave them to
themselves, and wait upon you.

Miss Moll grows a mighty beauty, and she shall be very prettily dressed, as likewise shall Betty and Eugene ; and, if I throw away a little money in adorning my brats, I hope you will forgive me. They are, I thank God, all very well ; and the charming form of their mother has tempered the likeness they bear to their rough sire, who is, with the greatest fondness, your most obliged and most obedient husband,

RICH. STEELE.

REAR-ADMIRAL SIR HORATIO NELSON TO LADY NELSON.

THESEUS, August, 1797.

I am so confident of your affection, that I feel the pleasure you will receive will be equal, whether my letter is wrote by my right hand or left. It was the chance of war, and I have great reason to be thankful ; and I know that it will add much to your pleasure in finding that Josiah, under God's Providence, was principally instrumental in saving my life. As to my health, it never was better; and now I hope soon to return to you ; and my Country, I trust, will not allow me any longer to linger in want of that pecuniary assistance which I have been fighting the whole war to preserve to her. But I shall not be surprised to be neglected and

forgot, as probably I shall no longer be considered as useful. However, I shall feel rich if I
continue to enjoy your affection. The cottage
is now more necessary than ever. You will see
by the papers, Lieutenant Weatherhead is
gone. Poor fellow! he lived four days after he
was shot. I shall not close this letter till I join
the Fleet, which seems distant; for it's been
calm these three days past. I am fortunate in
having a good surgeon on board; in short, I am
much more recovered than I could have expected. I beg neither you nor my father will
think much of this mishap : my mind has long
been made up to such an event. . . .

LORD EDWARD FITZGERALD TO HIS MOTHER.

FRESCATI, May 6, 1793.

Wife and I are come to settle here. We
came last night, got up to a delightful spring
day, and are now enjoying the little book-room,
with the windows open, hearing the birds sing,
and the place looking beautiful. The plants in
the passage are just watered ; and, with the passage door open, the room smells like a green-
house. Pamela has dressed four beautiful
flower-pots, and is now working at her frame,
while I write to my dearest mother ; and upon

the two little stands there are six pots of fine
auriculas, and I am sitting in the bay-window,
with all those pleasant feelings which the fine
weather, the pretty place, the singing birds, the
pretty wife, and Frescati give me,—with your
last dear letter to my wife before me :—so you
may judge how I love you at this moment.
Yes, dearest mother, I am delighted at the
Malvern party, and I am determined to meet
you there, or wherever you are. I dote on being with you anywhere, but particularly in the
country, as I think we always enjoy one another's company there more than in town. I
long for a little walk with you, leaning on me,
—or to have a long talk with you, sitting out
in some pretty spot, of a fine day, with your
long cane in your hand, working at some little
weed at your feet, and looking down, talking all
the time. . . .

MRS. RICHARD TRENCH TO ——— (A GOD-DAUGHTER).

April, 1821.

Excuse me for not having sooner expressed
the pleasure I felt in hearing of your being
well, and mother of a fine little boy. This is
the most delightful period of our existence ;
and when one forgets the little anxieties about

a baby's health, and the transient sufferings attendant upon their birth, often does one look back on those hours when infants were blossoming around one, with regret at their having so swiftly glided away. I believe it is the happiest time of every woman's life, who has affectionate feelings, and is blessed with healthy and well-disposed children. I know, at least, that neither the gayeties and boundless hopes of early life, nor the more grave pursuits and deeper affections of later years, are by any means comparable in my recollections with the serene yet lively pleasure of seeing my children—my beautiful, affectionate, and sprightly children—playing on the grass, enjoying their little temperate supper, or repeating " with holy look " their simple prayers, and undressing for bed, growing prettier for every part of their dress they took off, and at last lying down, all freshness and love, in complete happiness, and an amicable contest for mamma's last kiss.

THOMAS BABINGTON MACAULAY TO HIS MOTHER.

Trinity College, Cambridge, March 25, 1821.

. . . I entreat you to entertain no apprehensions about my health. My fever, cough, and

sore throat have all disappeared for the last
four days.   Many thanks for your intelligence
about poor dear John's recovery, which has
much exhilarated me. Yet I do not know
whether illness to him is not rather a preroga-
tive than an evil.   I am sure that it is well
worth while being sick to be nursed by a
mother.   There is nothing which I remember
with such pleasure as the time when you nursed
me at Aspenden.   The other night, when I lay
on my sofa very ill and hypochondriac, I was
thinking over that time.   How sick, and sleepless, and weak I was, lying in bed, when I was
told that you were come !   How well I remember with what an ecstasy of joy I saw that face
approaching me, in the middle of people that
did not care if I died that night except for the
trouble of burying me !   The sound of your
voice, the touch of your hand, are present to
me now, and will be, I trust in God, to my last
hour.   The very thought of these things in-
vigorated me the other day ; and I almost
blessed the sickness and low spirits which
brought before me associated images of a tenderness and an affection, which, however imperfectly repaid, are deeply remembered.   Such

scenes and such recollections are the bright half of human nature and human destiny. All objects of ambition, all rewards of talent, sink into nothing compared with that affection which is independent of good or adverse circumstances, excepting that it is never so ardent, so delicate, or so tender as in the hour of languor or distress. But I must stop. I had no intention of pouring out on paper what I am much more used to think than to express. Farewell, my dear Mother.

———

MARGARET CARLYLE TO THOMAS CARLYLE.

MAINHILL, March 21, 1821.

SON TOM:—I received your kind and pleasant letter. Nothing is more satisfying to me than to hear of your welfare. Keep up your heart, my brave boy. You ask kindly after my health. I complain as little as possible. When the day is cheerier, it has a great effect on me. But upon the whole I am as well as I can expect, thank God. I have sent a little butter and a few cakes with a box to bring home your clothes. Send them all home, that I may wash and sort them once more. Oh, man, could I but write! I 'll tell ye a' when we meet, but I must in the meantime content myself. Do send me a long letter; it revives me greatly; and tell me honestly if you read your chapter e'en and morn, lad. You mind I hod if not your hand, I hod your foot of it. Tell me if there is any thing you want in particular. I must run to pack the box, so I am

Your affectionate mother,
MARGARET CARLYLE.

THOMAS CARLYLE TO HIS MOTHER.

KINNAIRD HOUSE, June 10, 1823.

This letter may operate as a spur on the diligence of my beloved and valuable correspondents at Mainhill. There is a small blank made in the sheet for a purpose which you will notice.* I beg you to accept the little picture which fills it without any murmuring. It is a poor testimonial of the grateful love I should ever bear you. If I hope to get a moderate command of money in the course of my life's operations, I long for it chiefly that I may testify to those dear to me what affection I entertain for them. In the meantime we ought to

---

* Half a page is cut off, and contained evidently a check for a small sum of money.—J. A. FROUDE.

be thankful that we have never known what it
was to be in fear of want, but have always had
wherewith to gratify one another by these little
acts of kindness, which are worth more than
millions unblest by a true feeling between the
giver and receiver. You must buy yourself
any little odd things you want, and think I
enjoy it along with you, if it add to your comfort. I do indeed enjoy it with you. I should
be a dog if I did not. I am grateful to you
for kindness and true affection such as no other
heart will ever feel for me. I am proud of my
mother, though she is neither rich nor learned.
If I ever forget to love and reverence her, I
must cease to be a creature myself worth re-
membering. Often, my dear mother, in solitary, pensive moments does it come across me
like the cold shadow of death that we two
must part in the course of time. I shudder at
the thought, and find no refuge except in hum-
bly trusting that the great God will surely ap-
point us a meeting in that far country to which
we are tending. May he bless you forever, my
good mother, and keep up in your heart those
sublime hopes which at present serve as a pillar
of cloud by day and a pillar of fire by night to

guide your footsteps through the wilderness of life. We are in his hands. He will not utterly forsake us. Let us trust in him.

———

FALMOUTH, April 12, 1843.

I have just received my father's letter, which gives me at least the comfort of believing that you do not suffer very much pain. That your mind has remained so clear and strong, is an infinite blessing.

I do not know any thing in the world that would make up to me at all for wanting the recollection of the days I spent with you lately, when I was amazed at the freshness and life of all your thoughts. It brought back far distant years in the strangest, most peaceful way. I felt myself walking with you in Greenwich Park, and on the sea-shore at Sandgate ; almost even I seemed a baby with you bending over me. Dear Mother, there is surely something uniting us that cannot perish. I seem so sure of a love which shall last and reunite us, that even the remembrance, painful as that is, of all my own follies and ill-tempers, cannot shake this faith. When I think of you, and know how you feel towards me, and have felt for every moment of almost forty years, it would be too dark to believe that we shall never meet again. It was from you that I first learnt to think, to imagine, to believe; and these powers, which cannot be extinguished, will one day enter anew into communion with you. I have bought it very dear by the prospect of losing you in this world,—but since you have been so ill, every thing has seemed to me holier, loftier, and more lasting, more full of hope and final joy. . . .

LADY ELIZA CHANDOS TO HER DAUGHTER.*

Your letters by cousin Robert Serle arrived here not before the 27th of April, yet they were heartily welcome to us, bringing the joyful news, which a great while we had longed for, of my most dear mother and all other relations and friends good health, which I beseech God continue to you all, and as I observe in yours to your sister Betty the extraordinary kindness of (as I may truly say) the best mother and grandmother in the world in pinching herself to

* The young lady was living in England with her grandmother, Lady Bernard, her parents being in Constantinople, where Lord Chandos was the ambassador of King Charles II.

make you fine, so I cannot but admire her
great good housewifery in affording you so very
plentiful an allowance, and yet to increase her
stock at the rate I find she hath done; and
think I can never sufficiently mind you how
very much it is your duty on all occasions to
pay her your gratitude in all humble submission
and obedience to all her commands so long as
you live. I must tell you 't is to her bounty
and care in the greatest measure you are like to
owe your well-living in this world, and as you
cannot but be very sensible you are an extraordinary charge to her, so it behooves you to
take particular heed that in the whole course
of your life you render her a proportionate
comfort, especially since 't is the best way you
can ever hope to make her such amends as God
requires of your hands. But Poll! it grieves
me a little, and yet I am forced to take notice
of and reprove you for some vain expressions in
your letters to your sister—you say, concerning
your allowance: "you aim to bring your bread
and cheese even"; in this I do not discommend
you, for a foul shame indeed it would be should
you out-run the constable, having so liberal a
provision made you for your maintenance—but

the reason you give for your resolution I cannot at all approve; for you say: "to spend more you can't"—that's because you have it not to spend, otherwise it seems you would. So that 't is your grandmother's discretion and not yours that keeps you from extravagancy, which plainly appears in the close of your sentence, saying that you think it simple covetousness to save out of yours; but 't is my opinion if you lay all on your back 't is ten times a greater sin and shame than to save somewhat out of so large an allowance in your purse to help you at a dead lift. Child, we all know our beginning, but who knows his end? The best use that can be made of fair weather is to provide against foul; and 't is great discretion and no small commendations for a young woman betimes to show herself housewifely and frugal. Your mother, neither maid nor wife, ever yet bestowed forty pounds a year on herself, and yet if you never fall under a worse reputation in the world than she (I thank God for it) hath hitherto done, you need not repine at it; and you cannot be ignorant of the difference that was between my fortune and what you are to expect. You ought likewise to consider that you have seven brothers and sisters, and you are all one man's children, and therefore it is very unreasonable that one should expect to be preferred in finery so much above all the rest; for 't is impossible you should so much mistake your father's condition as to fancy that he is able to allow every one of you forty pounds a year, apiece; for such an allowance, with the charge of their diet over and above, will amount to at least five hundred pounds a year, a sum your poor father can ill spare; do but bethink yourself what a ridiculous sight it will be, when your grandmother and you come to us, to have no less than seven waiting-gentlewomen in one house,—for what reason can you give why every one of your sisters should not have every one of them a maid as well as you? and though you may spare to pay your maid's wages out of your allowance, yet you take no care of the unnecessary charge you put your father to in your increase of his family, whereas, if it were not a piece of pride to have the name of keeping your maid, she that waits on your good grandmother might easily do, as formerly you know she hath done, all the business you have for a maid, unless as you grow old you grow a verier fool—which God forbid!

Poll, you live in a place where you see great plenty and splendor, but let not the allurements of earthly pleasures tempt you to forget or neglect the duty of a good Christian in dressing your better part, which is your soul, as will best please God. I am not against your going decent and neat as becomes your father's daughter, but to clothe yourself rich and be running into every gaudy fashion can never become your circumstances, and instead of doing you credit and getting you a good preferent, it is the readiest way you can take to fright all sober men from ever thinking of matching themselves with women that live above their fortune; and if this be a wise way of spending money, judge you! And, besides, do but reflect what an odd sight it will be to a stranger that comes to our house, to see your grandmother, your mother, and all your sisters in a plain dress, and you only tricked up like a Bartlemew-babby—you know what sort of people those are that can't fare well but they must cry roast meat. Now what effect could you imagine your writing in such a high strain to your sisters could have, but either to provoke them to envy you or murmur against us? I must tell you, neither of your sisters have ever

had twenty pounds a year allowance from us
yet, and their dress hath not disparaged neither
them nor us; and without incurring the censure
of simple covetousness, they will have somewhat to show out of their saving that will do
them credit; and I expect that you, that are
their elder sister, should rather set them examples of the like nature than tempt them
from treading in the steps of their good grandmother and poor mother. This is not half
what might be said on this occasion, but believing thee to be a very good-natured, dutiful
child, I should have thought it a great deal too
much, but that having in my coming hither
past through many most desperate dangers, I
cannot forbear thinking and preparing myself
for all events; and, therefore, not knowing how
it may please God to dispose of us, I conclude
it my duty to God and thee, my dear child, to
lay this matter as home to thee as I could, as-
suring you my daily prayers are not nor shall
not be wanting that God may give you grace
always to remember to make a right use of this
truly affectionate counsel of your poor mother;
and though I speak very plain downright English to you, yet I would not have you doubt

but that I love you as heartily as any child I have, and if you serve God and take good courses I promise you my kindness to you shall be according to your own heart's desire; for you may be certain I can aim at nothing in what I have now writ but your real good, which to promote shall be the study and care day and night, of, my dear Poll, thy truly affectionate mother.

PERA OF GALATA, May 6, 1666.

———

BERNARD BARTON TO MRS. SUTTON.

WOODBRIDGE, July 26, 1839.

My dear good old mother's house is to be sold or offered by auction to-morrow. . . . The house, though very large and roomy, is near two hundred years old and copyhold, so not very salable, but sold on some terms it must and will be: so I turned into its old-fashioned garden the other day a young artist friend of mine, and sat him down on a stool in the middle of the long gravel walk leading from the parlor door to the bottom of the garden, which ends with a most beautiful and picturesque group of trees. These he has made a delightful water-color sketch of—an upright, about eleven inches high and eight wide. In the afternoon he turned his seat round, and sketched the back or garden in front of the house, as it looks from the garden, above, under, and through the trees. This drawing he has made as a companion to the Ive-Gill sketch he did me a short time ago, and the same size, ten inches by eight, so I have hung the trio over my study fire; and just under the tall upright one, I have hung the portrait of the old dear herself, . . . and a very pretty quartetto they make; the two garden scenes are such vivid transcripts of the spot depicted, and, though slight and free sketches only, retain so perfectly the spirit and character of the places that I could sit and look at them till I half fancy myself in the old familiar haunt; and the blessed old dear herself looks so perfectly at home, in the middle of her old and favorite garden, that it is quite a treat to look at her. Ive-Gill, I promise thee, is in goodly company, and becomes it well. Mother's house and garden were so old-fashioned, and the latter so wildly overgrown with trees, that they assort well together. Over the top of the house, as high as its towering chimney, is the tufted top of a tall sycamore, growing in the courtyard next the street: this, mother stuck in a twig, to tie a flower to, or point out where some seeds were sown, when she came home a bride near sixty-six or sixty-seven years ago. It took root, and is now a lofty tree, but one very likely to be cut down by some new owner, so I wished to preserve its memorial. But it is now break-fast time, and I have been scribbling this hour.

WILLIAM COWPER TO MRS. BODHAM.

WESTON, February 27, 1790.

My dearest Rose, whom I thought withered and fallen from the stalk, but whom I find still alive: nothing could give me greater pleasure than to know it, and to learn it from yourself. I loved you dearly when you were a child, and love you not a jot the less for having ceased to be so. Every creature that bears any affinity to my mother is dear to me, and you, the daughter of her brother, are but one remove distant from her: I love you, therefore, and love you much, both for her sake and for your own. The world could not have furnished you with a present so acceptable to me, as the pic-ture which you have so kindly sent me. I re-

ceived it the night before last, and viewed it
with a trepidation of nerves and spirits somewhat akin to what I should have felt had the
dear original presented herself to my embraces.
I kissed it, and hung it where it is the last object that I see at night, and, of course, the first
on which I open my eyes in the morning. She
died when I completed my sixth year; yet I
remember her well, and am an ocular witness of
the great fidelity of the copy. I remember,
too, a multitude of the maternal tendernesses
which I received from her, and which have endeared her memory to me beyond expression.
There is in me, I believe, more of the Donne
than of the Cowper; and though I love all of
both names, and have a thousand reasons to
love those of my own name, yet I feel the bond
of nature draw me vehemently to your side. I
was thought in the days of my childhood much
to resemble my mother; and in my natural
temper, of which at the age of fifty-eight I
must be supposed to be a competent judge, can
trace both her and my late uncle, your father.
Somewhat of his irritability, and a little, I
would hope, both of his and of her——, I
know not what to call it, without seeming to

praise myself, which is not my intention, but speaking to *you*, I will even speak out, and say *good nature.* Add to all this, I deal much in poetry, as did our venerable ancestor, the Dean of St. Paul's, and I think I shall have proved myself a Donne at all points. The truth is that, whatever I am, I love you all. . . .

BERNARD BARTON TO CHARLES TAYLOR.

WOODBRIDGE, April 22, 1824.

My head and heart are full even to over-flowing: my eyes are almost dim with gazing at one object, yet are still unsatisfied. I keep thinking of one thing all day, stealing to feast my eyes on it when I can, and lie down to dream of it o' nights. In one sentence, my good cousins at Carlisle have sent me my dear, dear father's picture. It is in most excellent preservation, not at all injured by the journey, and I write to-night to a friend in town to arrange for its being neatly framed. But I must describe it.

Its size is about four and a half by rather more than three and a half feet;—how I wish our parlor were a little larger! My dear *pater* is seated at a round table, his elbow resting on

it, and his right hand as if partly supporting
his head; the little finger folded down, the two
fore ones extended up to his temple. Before
him is a sheet of paper, headed "Abstract of
Locke"; the chapter on Perception, and the
first volume of Locke, open, is on his left hand,
on his knee. His countenance is full of
thought, yet equally full of sweetness. What
an ugly fellow I am compared to him! A little
farther on the table is a German flute, and a
piece of Handel's music, open, leaning against
Akenside's "Pleasures of Imagination." A larger
volume also lies on the table, lettered "Ken-
drick's Dictionary," and several letters, the
date of one of which, at the bottom, is March,
1774. (I conclude the picture was painted
then.) In the corner, just below the table,
stands a globe. On the book-shelves behind
him are, first, a volume—the first line of the
title I can't make out—"on Euclid"; then,
I think, "Simpson's Algebra," "Fitzosborne's
Letters," another book lettered, I think, "Ver-
ulam," "Fordyce," "Pope's Works," "Dictionary of Arts and Sciences," two or three
volumes. The titles of the upper row of books
are hid by a sort of curtain. An open window
on the other side of the table gives a peep of

sunset sky. His dress is a suit of so red a
brown as almost to approach crimson; his
hair turned back from a fine clear forehead,
with a curl over each ear, and tied in a sort of
club behind; the ruffles at his wrists, as well as
a frill, to say nothing of the flute, show that he
had not then joined the Quakers. His age
when this picture was taken I suppose was
about twenty. I think I understand it was the
year before his marriage. His countenance
is all I could wish it—(delicately fair, which I
had always heard, and rather small features),—
in the bloom of youth, yet thoughtful—*to me*
full of intellect and benignity. O how proud
I am of him!—how thankful I am that I have
written what good-natured critics call poetry!
for to my poetical fame, humble as it is, I owe
the possession of this, to me, inestimable treasure. It has put me all but beside myself; I
go and look at it, then stand a little farther off,
then nearer, then try it in a new light—then go
to the street door to see if anybody be in sight
who can at all value its beauties, and enter into
my feelings—if so, I lug them in, incontinently.
My good mother-in-law, I mean my wife's
mother, a plain, excellent Quaker lady, who, I
dare say, never *went anywhere* to look at a

picture before, has been to see it; she thinks she sees a likeness to my girl in it. I wish I could—but I quite encourage her in doing so: my girl will never be half so handsome, though far more personable than her father. But she cannot come up to her grandfather. I must stop somewhere, so I may as well now. I make no excuses; I will not so far affront *thee*. I conjecture what thy feelings would be hadst thou lost a father at the age I was when deprived of mine, hadst thou always heard him spoken of as one of the most amiable, and intelligent, and estimable of men, yet been unable to picture to thyself what his outward semblance was;—then thirty years and more after his death, to hear that a portrait of him, stated by those who knew him to be a likeness, was in existence, yet almost to despair of ever seeing it, without travelling hundreds of miles —I, too, who have little more locomotion than a cabbage; and after all to be its possessor!

———

LEIGH HUNT TO HIS SON, VINCENT LEIGH HUNT.

KENSINGTON, June 21, 1843.

MY DEAR BOY:—No two persons, I think, in the world understand one another's feelings

better than you and I ; so pray be always quite
at your ease with respect to what you do or do
not do in regard to writing ; for I shall always
put it to its right account, and know that you
are acting towards me in the most delicate and
conscientious manner. When your letter came
yesterday I was in the act of going out in a
hurry, by omnibus : so, after ascertaining that
all was well, I put it in my pocket, and did
not read it till I was in the midst of the bustle
of the Strand. In a moment I was in the
thick of the solitude with you, looking at the
old church and the woodman, and hearing " the
blessed silence." It is curious to reflect how
totally one can be absorbed, and afar off, on
these occasions (for I was literally so), and yet
go on, in and out, among a crowd of people.
How it rejoices me to see you realizing thus
something of your day-dreams, and, above all,
getting better health. I think of you very
often ; and wish you by me, and yet I think I
could miss you a good half year, or even more,
provided you came back plump and jovial. I
am going out again this morning to see Webster, who was not in town yesterday, and the
hurry makes me write this scrawl, but I am re-

solved not to lose another post. Love to all, and tell Jace, with a kiss, that I will write to her again when she does to her and your most loving father.

———

NORMAN MACLEOD TO HIS SON.

GLASGOW, August 4, 1862.

I am so glad you are in Morven, and so happy there. I never was so happy in all my life as I used to be when I was a boy there. I think of you as if you were myself young again. For I fished with Sandy and Uncle John for cod among the rocks in the bay, and in the burn for trout, and went to the Byre for warm milk, just as you are doing. But then all the old terriers are dead. There were Cuilag and Gasgach—oh, such dogs! If you saw them worry an otter or wild-cat! They would never give in. Ask your Uncle John about them, and ask him to show you the otter's den at Clachoran. O Nommey, be happy! for when you are old like me you will remember Fiunary as if it was the Garden of Eden, without the serpent.

I wish you could remember, as I can, all the dear friends who were once there, and who would have loved you as they loved me—my grandpa, with his white hair and blind eyes, and my grandmamma so kind and loving, and aunts Margaret, Mary, Grace, Archy, Jessy. I see all their faces now before me. They were all so good, and loved God and everybody. Dockie, dear! thank God for good friends, and for having so many of them.

Did they show you where I lived when I was a boy, and the school I used to be in? . . .

———

NORMAN MACLEOD TO HIS DAUGHTER (UPON HER FIRST LEAVING HOME TO GO TO SCHOOL).

GLASGOW, April 30, 1865.

. . . So you were very sorry, old girl, when we left you that day? You thought you would not care. Hem! I knew better.

And so the poor lassie cried, and was so lonely the first night, and would have given worlds to be at home again! And your old dad was not a bit sorry to leave you, not he— cruel-hearted man that he is! Nor was your mother, wretched old woman that she is! And yet " you would wonder " how sorry we both were, and how often the old man said " Poor dear darling!" But no tear filled our eye.

Are you sure of that? I 'm not. And the
old father said: "I 'm not afraid of my girl.
I 'm sure she will prove herself good, kind,
loving, and obedient, and won't be lazy, but do
her work like a heroine, and remember all her old
dad told her!" and her mammy said the same.
And then the mammy would cry, and the old
dad would call her a fool (respectfully). And
so we reached London, and then we got your
letter, which made us very happy, and then the
old man said: " Never fear! she will do right
well, and will be very happy, and Miss ——
will like her, and she will like Miss ——!" and
"We shall soon meet again!" chimed in the
mammy. " If it be God's will we shall,"
said the dad, "and won't we be happy!"

God bless you, my darling! May you love
your own Father in heaven far more than you
love your own father on earth, and I know how
truly you love me, and you know how truly I
love you; but He loves you infinitely more
than I can possibly do, though I give you my
whole heart.

Will you write a line to the old man? And,
remember, he won't criticise it, but be glad to
hear all your chatter.

THOMAS DE QUINCEY TO MISS MARY RUSSEL MITFORD.

LASSWADE, 1842.

. . . More pleasant it must be if I try to give you some clue to the motive, the how and the why, of my residence in this place. My companions, as you know, are my three daughters, who, if it should be found that they had no other endowment from the bounty of nature, have this one, perhaps better than all that I could ask for them from the most potent of fairies, viz.: that they live in the most absolute harmony I have ever witnessed. Such a sound as that of dissension in any shade or degree I have not once heard issuing from their lips. And it gladdens me beyond measure that all day long I hear from their little drawing-room intermitting sounds of gayety and laughter, the most natural and spontaneous. Three sisters more entirely loving to each other, and more unaffectedly drawing their daily pleasures from sources that will always continue to lie within their power—viz.: books and music,—I have not either known or heard of. Our dwelling is a little cottage, containing eight rooms only, one of which (the largest), or what in London is called the *first* floor, is used as a drawing-room, and one about half the size, on the ground-floor, a dining-room, but for a party of ten people at the utmost. Our garden gate is exactly seven measured miles from the Scott Monument in Princes Street, Edinburgh. Lasswade, to which nominally we allocate ourselves, is in fact one mile and a half distant; but, as it is the nearest town possessing a market and a regular post-office (Dalkeith, which is very much larger, being distant three and a half miles or more), and as our means of communicating with Lasswade, though imperfect enough, are better than with any other place, it follows that Lasswade is the best address. . . . We keep only two servants (female servants), a housemaid and a cook, and with so narrow a command of labor, we are unable to send for our letters, the journey to and fro making a clear total of three miles' walking.

JULIUS HARE TO FRANCIS HARE.

HURSTMONCEAUX, March 6, 1834.

It is very, very long since I wrote to you. I began a letter to you indeed this day two months, but I could not finish it. All other feelings of late have been swallowed up in anx-

iety about Augustus, and I have scarcely
written to any one except about him, and to
those who could give me the most accurate details. To-day, however, when I have learnt that
we have lost him forever in this world, I feel a
longing to tighten the tie with those brothers
who are still left to me; and while I have been
thinking over all I had, and all I have lost, in
him, I have also called to mind what I still
have in my other brothers. How much, dearest
Francis, do I owe to you. How much have I
owed to you ever since my earliest years.
How patient you were with me; how indulgent; what pains you took with me; how you
gave up your time to me! What unvarying,
unmerited kindness have you shown me all my
life long! And though we have been so much
separated by circumstances of late years, and
though my negligence has often let a very
long period pass without any communication
between us, the fault has been entirely on my
side, and I found last year at Naples that your
affection was as strong as ever. Such indeed,
has always been my situation, that I have constantly been the receiver of kindnesses from
all my brothers, and have hardly ever been
able to do any thing in return. I can merely

acknowledge and feel grateful for them. And
to-day has re-enlivened my gratitude to you,
and makes me anxious to assure you that all
your goodness has not been thrown away on
one who is utterly unmindful of it. I want,
too, to thank you for all your kindness and
attention to Augustus. Alas, that I could do
nothing for him! But you and Marcus have
fulfilled my share of his nursing as well as your
own, and nothing in this respect seems to have
been wanting. Still, I can hardly bring myself
to believe that our brotherhood has lost its
heavenliest flower. It seemed to be such an
essential part of one's self. I could never conceive myself as living without my three
brothers, and almost fancied that time could
have no power over a bond so strong in affection. God grant that the same bond which
has existed here on earth, and which has now
begun to dissolve, may hereafter be united
again in still stronger affection in heaven!

THOMAS CARLYLE TO HIS BROTHER ALEXANDER
CARLYLE.

EDINBURGH, December 5, 1820.

I sit down with the greatest pleasure to
answer your most acceptable letter. The warm

affection, the generous sympathy displayed in it go near the heart, and shed over me a meek and kindly dew of brotherly love more refreshing than any but a wandering, forlorn mortal can well imagine. Some of your expressions affect me almost to weakness—I might say, with pain, if I did not hope the course of events will change our feelings from anxiety to congratulation, from soothing adversity to adorning prosperity. I marked your disconsolate look. It has often since been painted in the mind's eye ; but believe me, my boy, these days will pass over. We shall all get to rights in good time, and, long after, cheer many a winter evening by recalling such pensive, but yet amiable and manly, thoughts to our minds. And in the meanwhile let me utterly sweep away the vain fear of our forgetting one another. There is less danger of this than of any thing. We Carlyles are a clannish people, because we have all something original in our formation, and find therefore less than common sympathy with others ; so that we are constrained, as it were, to draw to one another, and to seek that friendship in our own blood which we do not find so readily elsewhere.

Jack and I and you will respect one another to the end of our lives, because I predict that our conduct will be worthy of respect, and we will love one another, because the feelings of our young days—feelings impressed most deeply on the young heart—are all intertwined and united by the tenderest yet strongest ties of our nature. But independently of this your fear is in vain. Continue to cultivate your abilities, and to behave steadily and quietly as you have done, and neither of the two literati * are likely to find many persons more qualified to appreciate their feelings than the farmer their brother. Greek words and Latin are fine things, but they cannot hide the emptiness and lowness of many who employ them. . . .

THOMAS CARLYLE TO HIS BROTHER JOHN CARLYLE.

CHELSEA, September 21, 1834.

Your kind letter, my dear Jack, was read over with a feeling such as it merited ; it went nearer my heart than any thing addressed to me for long. I am not sure that there were not *tears* in the business, but they were not sad ones.

* His brother John and himself.

Your offers and purposes are worthy of a brother, and I were but unworthy if I met them in any mean spirit. I believe there is no other man living from whom such offers as yours were other to me than a pleasant sound which I *must disregard ;* but it is not so with these; for I actually can (without damage to any good feeling in me), and will, if need be, make good use of them. We will, as you say, stand by one another ; and so each of us, were all other men arranged against us, have one good friend. Well that it is so. *Wohl ihm dem die Geburt den Bruder gab.* I will not speak any more about this, but keep it laid up in my mind as a thing to act by. I feel, as I once said, *double*-strong in the possession of my poor *Doil,** and so I suppose we shall quarrel many times yet, and instantly agree again, and argue and sympathize, and on the whole stand by one another through good and evil, and turn *two* fronts to the world while we are both spared in it. *Amen !* There are many wallowing in riches, splendent in dignities, who have no such possession as this. Let us be thankful for it, and approve ourselves worthy of it. . . .

---

* A family nickname for his brother.

FRANCIS JEFFREY TO HIS DAUGHTER.

CRAIGCROOK, Sunday, May 23, 1847.

Bless you ever! And this is my first right
earnest, tranquil, Sunday blessing since my return; for the day after my arrival I was in a
worry with heaps of unanswered letters and
neglected arrangements. But to-day I got
back to my old Sabbath feeling of peace, love,
and seclusion. Granny has gone to church,
and the babes and doggies are walking, and I
have paced leisurely round my garden, to the
songs of hundreds of hymning blackbirds and
thrushes, and stepped stately along my terrace,
among the bleaters in the lawn below, and possessed my heart in quietness, and felt that
there was sweetness in solitude, and that the
world, whether to be left, or to be yet awhile
lived in, is a world to be loved, and only to be
enjoyed by those who find objects of love in it.
And this is the sum of the matter, and the
first and last and only enduring condition of all
good people, when their fits of vanity and ambition are off them, or finally sinking to repose.
Well, but here has been Tarley, come of her
own sweet will, to tell me with a blush and a
smile, and ever so little of a stammer, that she

would like if I would walk with her, and we
have been walking, hand in hand, down to the
bottom of the quarry, where the water is growing, though slowly, and up to the Keith's
sweetbriar alley, very sweet and resonant with
music of birds, and rich with cowslips and
orchis, and over the stile back to our domains,
and been sitting in the warm corner by the gardener's house, and taking cognizance of the
promise of gooseberries and currants, of which
we are to have pies, I think, next week, and
gazing at the glorious brightness of the gen-
tians, and the rival brightness of the peacock's neck, and discoursing of lambs and children, and goodness and happiness, and their
elements and connections. Less discussion,
though, than usual, in our Sunday Tusculans,
and more simple chat, as from one friend to
another. And now she has gone to sharpen
her teeth for dinner, and tell as much as she
likes of our disceptations, and I come back to
my letter. We met the boy and Ali early in our
ramble, and he took my other hand for a while;
but Ali would not trust him in the quarry, and
so we parted—on the brink of perdition,—and
he roared lustily at sight of our peril.

FRANCIS JEFFREY TO HIS GRANDCHILD.

CRAIGCROOK, June 20, 1848.

MY SONSY NANCY :—I love you very much, and think very often of your dimples, and your pimples ; and your funny little plays, and all your pretty ways ; and I send you my blessing, and wish I were kissing your sweet rosy lips, or your fat finger tips ; and that you were here, so that I could hear your stammering words, from a mouthful of curds ; and a great purple tongue (as broad as it 's long ;) and see your round eyes, open wide with surprise, and your wondering look, to find yourself at Craigcrook ! To-morrow is Maggie's *birthday*, and we have built up a great bonfire in honor of it ; and Maggie Rutherfurd (do you remember her at all ?) is coming out to dance round it ; and all the servants are to drink her health, and wish her many happy days with you and Frankie ; and all the mammys and pappys, whether grand or not grand. We are very glad to hear that she and you love each other so well, and are happy in making each other happy ; and that you do not forget dear Tarley or Frankie, when they are out of sight, nor Granny either—or even old Granny pa, who is

in most danger of being forgotten, he thinks.
We have had showery weather here, but the
garden is full of flowers; and Frankie has a new
wheel-barrow, and does a great deal of work,
and *some mischief* now and then. All the dogs
are well; and Foxy is mine, and Froggy is
Tarley's, and Frankie has taken up with great
white Neddy—so that nothing is left for Granny but old barking Jackey and Dover when the
carriage comes. The donkey sends his compliments to you, and maintains that you are a
cousin of his! or a near relation, at all events.
He wishes, too, that you and Maggie would
come, for he thinks that you will not be so
heavy on his back as Tarley and Maggie
Rutherfurd, who now ride him without mercy.
This is Sunday, and Ali is at church—Granny
and I taking care of Frankie till she comes
back, and he is now hammering very busily at
a corner of the carpet, which he says does not
lie flat. He is very good, and really too pretty
for a boy, though I think his two eyebrows are
growing into one—stretching and meeting each
other above his nose! But he has not near so
many *freckles* as Tarley—who has a fine crop of
them—which she and I encourage as much as

we can.   I hope you and Maggie will lay in a
stock of them, as I think no little girl can be
pretty without them in summer.   Our pea-hens
are suspected of having young families in some
hiding-place, for, though they pay us short
visits now and then, we see them but seldom,
and always alone.   If you and Maggie were
here with your sharp eyes, we think you might
find out their secrets and introduce us to a nice
new family of young peas.   The old papa cock,
in the meantime, says he knows nothing about
them, and does not care a farthing! We envy
you your young peas of another kind, for we
have none yet, nor any asparagus either, and
hope you will bring some down to us in your
lap.   Tarley sends her love, and I send mine to
you all ; though I shall think most of Maggie
to-morrow morning, and of you when your
birth-morning comes.   When is that, do you
know? It is never dark now, here, and we might
all go to bed without candles.   And so bless
you ever and ever, my dear, dimply pussie.

———

CATHERINE STANLEY TO HER SISTER.
ALDERLEY, 1818.

. . . How I have enjoyed these fine days,—
and one's pleasure is doubled, or, rather, I should

say trebled, in the enjoyment of the three little children basking in the sunshine on the lawns, and picking up daisies, and finding new flowers every day,—and in seeing Arthur * expand like one of the flowers in the fine weather. Owen trots away to school at nine o'clock every morning, with his Latin grammar under his arm, leaving Mary with a strict charge to unfurl his flag, which he leaves carefully furled, through the little Gothic gate, as soon as the clock strikes twelve. So Mary unfurls the flag, and then watches till Owen comes in sight, and as soon as he spies her signal, he sets off full gallop towards her, and Mary creeps through the gate to meet him, and then comes with as much joy to announce Owen's being come back, as if he was returned from the North Pole. Meanwhile I am sitting with the doors open into the trellis, so that I can see and hear all that passes. . . .

———

ROBERT SOUTHEY TO GROSVENOR C. BEDFORD.

Keswick, July 29, 1820.

It is very seldom that a whole month elapses without some interchange of letters between

* The future Dean Stanley.

you and me ; and, for my part, in the present
instance, I cannot plead any unusual press of
business, or any remarkable humor of industry.
But then I can plead a great deal of enjoyment.
I have been staying in the house all day—a
great happiness after the hard service upon
which my ten trotters were continually kept in
London. I have been reading—a great luxury
for one who during eleven weeks had not half
an hour for looking through a book. I have
been playing with Cuthbert, giving him the
Cries of London to the life, as the accompani-
ment to a series of prints thereof, and enacting
lion, tiger, bull, bear, horse, ass, elephant, rhi-
noceros, the laughing hyena, owl, cuckoo, peacock, turkey-cock, raven, magpie, cock, duck,
and goose, etc., greatly to his delight and somewhat to his edification, for never was there a
more apt and willing pupil. Whenever he
comes near the study door, he sets up a shout,
which seldom fails of producing an answer ; in
he comes, tottering along with a smile upon his
face, and *pica pica* in his mouth ; and if the
picture-book is not forthwith forthcoming, he
knows its place upon the shelf, and uses most
ambitious and persevering efforts to drag out a

folio. And if this is not a proper excuse for idleness, Grosvenor, what is ? . . .

KESWICK, November 11, 1814.

. . . Neville was more fortunate than you in his excursion to this land of loveliness. He had delightful weather, and he made the most of it. Never had we a more indefatigable guest, nor one who enjoyed the country more heartily. Since his return, Neville-like, he has loaded us with presents; and no children were ever happier than these young ones were when the expected box made its appearance. I happened to be passing the evening at the island with General Peachey when it arrived, and they one and all laid their injunctions upon their mother not to tell me what each had received, that they might surprise me with the sight in the morning. Accordingly, no sooner was my door opened in the morning than the whole swarm were in an uproar, buzzing about me. In an evil moment I had begun to shave myself; before the operation was half over, Edith, with her work-box, was on one side, Herbert, with his books, on the other, and little Isabel, jig-

ging for delight, in the midst of them, was crying out *mine—mine—Mitter White*—and holding up a box of Tunbridge ware. My poor
chin suffered for all this, and the scene would
have made no bad subject for Wilkie or Bird.
God bless you!

MISS MARY RUSSEL MITFORD TO MISS EMILY
JEPHSON.

June 23, 1854.

. . . Little Miss Mary is a great comfort and
delight. Your charming description of Miss
Emily would almost serve for her—she is the
brightest, merriest, happiest creature that ever
existed—knowing fewer words, I think, than
six months ago. You know she was a year old
the second of last January, but everybody
takes her for a twelvemonth older—she is so
tall, so large, and so active, understanding everybody, and making herself understood in spite
of her want of language. Such a mimic never
was seen. She comes to my door knocking
with her little clenched fist every time she can
escape from her father and mother and the
maid; and in imitation, we suppose, of her
brother, folds her little hands every night and
says, " Bless papa and mamma and poor *Ba*,"

the hideous name (nobody can guess why) she will call me. She knows all my things for use or wearing, and is furiously angry if any thing she has been accustomed to see in my room meets her eye out of it. "Ba's," she says upon such occasions. "Poor Ba's," "My Ba's." In the same way she brings me all newspapers, letters, flowers, and books, and would certainly fight for the possession of a letter especially, which it is her great delight to deliver with her own hand. I suppose she is pretty, everybody says so—colored like certain balsams and carnations, with the skin of the texture of a rose-leaf, exquisite blue eyes, a merry, round face, a little figure admirably formed with dimples instead of joints, and lovely golden hair curling round her white neck and two or three shades lighter than her long eyelashes. How I wish I could see you, my dearest, and that we could compare our pets! . . .

LADY SIDNEY OWENSON MORGAN TO HER SISTER.

Chateau de la Grange, September 10, 1818.

Nothing can equal our uneasiness at not hearing from you. We lingered in Paris day after day, still expecting a letter and good news,

until General La Fayette wrote to us to say
how anxiously we were expected here this some
time back; and in the hope that your letter
would follow us immediately, we set off for La
Grange, Mr. Warden, our American friend, having taken charge of all our letters, which he is
to forward us as they arrive . . . Nothing
could equal the kindness, cordiality, and affection of our reception here. We found the general younger by a dozen years; another grandchild, making twelve, in addition to his family;
also a delightful old lady, Madame la Comtesse
de Tracy, whose brother, Monsieur de Scoval,
married a sister of Lord Kinnaird's, and whose
daughter is married to young La Fayette, the
colonel; but her greatest illustration is that
she is the wife of one of the most eminent men
and celebrated metaphysicians in France. A
very clever young artist, who is painting the
general's picture, Monsieur Scheffer; and one
of the most delightful musicians I ever heard,
a Monsieur Carbonel, whose playing and singing is such a treat to Morgan that he keeps him
to it from morning till night. He goes through
whole operas, and his French songs would delight you as much as Moore's. He is a charming composer, and seems partly amateur, partly

professional: he assists in the academy of the children—for it is literally an academy,—as does also Monsieur Scheffer. There are, besides, in the house a music-master and an English governess. Before breakfast I find all the young people at their easels painting from models in the anteroom; then they go to their music (there are three pianos); then they all turn out into the beautiful park for two hours, and then resume their studies for two hours more. But I never saw such happy children; they live without restraint, and, except while at their lessons, always with the grown people. If the little ones are noisy, they are sent into the anteroom; but their gentleness and good conduct are astonishing, considering, too, that eleven of the twelve are always with us. Oscar and Octavie, a little boy and girl of three and four years old, are great friends of mine. Octavie puts me so much in mind of darling baby that I have her often with me. She said yesterday to her mamma, " J'ai cherché une rose pour cette petite dame, qui est si bonne pour moi, mais le jardinier m'a fermé le grille (the garden gate) au nez "; would you not be surprised at such a gallantry on the part of Miss Baby? it amused me much, as being so French. But the children are amazingly forward here; they breakfast, dine, and sup with us, and nothing amuses me more than to see them conversing with all their little airs and graces, and not the least noisy. What would amuse you most is to see them breakfasting on soup, made dishes, and drinking Burgundy after it; it is a knock-down to all Morgan's arguments and mine. Morgan breakfasts like the rest; but I have coffee, by particular desire, after breakfast. Every one drinks tea and coffee as after dinner; and though this substantial meal is taken at ten o'clock, every one is ready for the abundant and excellent dinner which is served at four; coffee comes immediately after, and tea at ten. I never saw such a beautiful picture of domestic happiness, virtue, and talent. The general has proposed inviting Humboldt and Dénon to join us. If they come, Europe could scarcely present such another circle of talent and celebrity.

FRANCIS JEFFREY TO HIS SON-IN-LAW WILLIAM EMPSON.

CRAIGCROOK, Sunday, May 30, 1846.

Bless you all my darlings! and keep you well, and loving, and happy! The world looks

happy here, this morning, for May is going out
rather more like herself than she came in, or
has hitherto progressed. There was a glorious
moon last night and a bright sun this morning,
and the thermometer is up to sixty-two (which,
as it is only ten o'clock yet, we think a great
deal), and there is but little wind, and the grass
is of a deeper green, and the new leafing of the
trees so light, and tender, and graceful, and the
sheep so well washed by the thunder-showers
of yesterday morning, so white and foam-like,
as they lie in tufts on the lawn, and the boy is
full of egg, and Tarley of bacon, and Granny
does not go to church, but Ali instead, and the
horses and donkey, too, have a holiday, and we
have no spite, or envy, or ambition among us,
and no pains (to speak of) in our bodies, and no
remorses, or ennuis, or want of alacrity in our
minds, and so we have reason, I think, for
thankfulness and content. . . .

FRIENDSHIP.

CHARLOTTE BRONTE TO W. S. WILLIAMS.

HAWORTH, July 21, 1851.

. . . I could not help wondering whether Cornhill will ever change for me, as Oxford has changed for you. I have some pleasant associations connected with it now—will these alter their character some day?

Perhaps they may—though I have faith to the contrary, because, I *think*, I do not exaggerate my partialities; I *think* I take faults along with excellences — blemishes together with beauties. And, besides, in the matter of friendship, I have observed that disappointment here arises chiefly, *not* from liking our friends too well, or thinking of them too highly, but rather from an over-estimate of *their* liking for and opinion of *us;* and that if we guard ourselves with sufficient scrupulousness of care from error in this direction, and can be con-

tent and even happy to give more affection
than we receive—can make just comparison of
circumstances, and be severely accurate in drawing inferences thence, and never let self-love
blind our eyes,—I think we may manage to get
through life with consistency and constancy,
unembittered by that misanthropy which springs
from revulsions of feeling. All this sounds a
little metaphysical, but it is good sense if you
consider it. The moral of it is, that if we
would build on a sure foundation in friendship,
we must love our friends for *their* sakes rather
than for *our own;* we must look at their truth
to *themselves*, full as much as their truth to
us. In the latter case, every wound to self-
love would be a cause of coldness ; in the
former, only some painful change in the
friend's character and disposition—some fearful breach in his allegiance to his better self—
could alienate the heart. . . .

WILLIAM COWPER TO WILLIAM UNWIN.

OLNEY, October 5, 1780.

. . . Connections formed at school are said
to be lasting, and often beneficial. There are
two or three stories of this kind upon record,

which would not be so constantly cited as they are, whenever this subject happens to be mentioned, if the chronicle that preserves their remembrance had many besides to boast of. For my own part, I found such friendships, though warm enough in their commencement, surprisingly liable to extinction ; and of seven or eight, whom I had selected for intimates out of about three hundred, in ten years' time not one was left me. The truth is, that there may be, and often is, an attachment of one boy to another, that looks very like a friendship ; and while they are in circumstances that enable them mutually to oblige and to assist each other promises well, and bids fair to be lasting. But they are no sooner separated from each other, by entering into the world at large, than other connections, and new employments, in which they no longer share together, efface the remembrance of what passed in earlier days, and they become strangers to each other for ever. Add to this, that the *man* frequently differs so much from the *boy*,—his principles, manners, temper, and conduct, undergo so great an alteration,—that we no longer recognize in him our old playfellow, but find him utterly unworthy and unfit for the place he once held in our affections. . . .

MISS CHARLOTTE BRONTE TO MISS WOOLER.

HAWORTH, September 27, 1850.

. . . You say you suspect I have formed a large circle of acquaintance by this time. No; I cannot say that I have. I doubt whether I possess either the wish or the power to do so. A few friends I should like to have, and these few I should like to know well; if such knowledge brought proportionate regard, I could not help concentrating my feelings; dissipation, I think, appears synonymous with dilution. However, I have, as yet, scarcely been tried. During the month I spent in London in the spring, I kept very quiet, having the fear of lionizing before my eyes. I only went out once to dinner; and once was present at an evening party; and the only visits I have paid have been to Sir James Kay Shuttleworth's and my publisher's. From this system I should not like to depart; as far as I can see, indiscriminate visiting tends only to a waste of time, and a vulgarizing of character. . . .

BERNARD BARTON TO GEORGE CRABBE.

WOODBRIDGE, August 20, 1846.

I was going to begin " My dear old Friend," for I have sometimes hard work to convince myself that our acquaintance is only of a few years' standing. There are natures so intrenched in all sorts of artificial outworks, each of which must be deliberately carried by siege ere you can get at what there is of nature in them, that you had need *know* them, in conventional phraseology, half or a quarter of a life, ere you know aught about them. There are others whom, by a sort of instinctive free-masonry, you seem old friends with at once. The value of the acquisition depends not always on the time and labor it costs to make it—it is very often clean the contrary; for it by no means unfrequently turns out that what has cost you much time and pains to get at is worth little when obtained. I speak not of principles or truths, which you must find out for yourself, and this must often be a slow process; but I am talking of those who profess them, and these, methinks, ought to be more promptly discernible and discoverable. Man would not be such a riddle to man did not too many of us wear

masks, and intrench ourselves in all sorts of con-
ventionalities and formalities. I do not think
there is much of these in either of *us ;* and that,
I take it, is the reason why we have got all the
more readily at each other. Enough, however,
of this long introduction, which I have blundered
into without design or malice aforethought. . . .

JOHN KEATS TO BENJAMIN BAILEY.

January 23, 1818.

. . . Things have happened lately of great
perplexity; you must have heard of them;
Reynolds and Haydon retorting and recrimi-
nating, and parting forever. The same thing has
happened between Haydon and Hunt. It is
unfortunate; men should bear with each other;
there lives not the man who may not be cut up,
aye, lashed to pieces, on his weakest side. The
best of men have but a portion of good in them
—a kind of spiritual yeast in their frames, which
creates the ferment of existence—by which a
man is propelled to act, and strive, and buffet
with circumstance. The sure way, Bailey, is
first to know a man's faults, and then be passive.
If, after that, he insensibly draws you towards
him, then you have no power to break the link.
Before I felt interested in either Reynolds or

Haydon, I was well-read in their faults; yet, knowing them, I have been cementing gradually with both. I have an affection for them both, for reasons almost opposite; and to both must I of necessity cling, supported always by the hope that when a little time, a few years, shall have tried me more fully in their esteem, I may be able to bring them together. The time must come, because they have both hearts; and they will recollect the best parts of each other, when this gust is overblown. . . .

BISHOP CONNOP THIRLWALL TO ——

ABERGWILI, New Year's Day, 1867.

I had fully intended to gild and sweeten the close of the old year for myself by a letter which you should receive this day; but wishing first to be at liberty from official business, I had to plunge into the thicket of correspondence, from which, as it turned out, I could not extricate myself until it was too near post-time to begin the only letter which I really desired to write. I have now the advantage of being able to send you the wishes of the New Year without forestalling the future. But words cannot convey the feeling with which they spring from my heart, so as to distinguish them from conventional complimentary phrases.

You must give me credit for a great deal more than language can express. Though not in accordance with common practice, it will be a surer proof of my regard for you if I take you to task, and scold you a little this New Year's Day, in the hope that you will now turn over a new leaf, and break yourself of the only fault that I have hitherto been able to perceive in you.

It is not that which you lay to your own charge, but rather just the reverse. You talk of *distrusting* yourself, and this is evidently a cause of real unhappiness to you. But the fact is that you trust yourself a great deal too much, while in exactly the same degree you distrust all your best friends. Will you never be persuaded to rely a little less upon your own judgment and to place a little more confidence in theirs? Is it not presumptuous to set up your own opinion against one in which they are unanimously opposed to it?

Why will you think so lightly of them as not to give them credit for being able to discern your character better than you can yourself? Is it not universally admitted that to know

one's self is the most difficult of all things, and
that if we differ in our appreciation from those
who have the best opportunities of knowing
what we really are, it is quite certain that they
are in the right and we in the wrong? Why
will you insist on making yourself out to be an
exception to the rule, and keep on suspecting
and accusing yourself, when all your friends are
thoroughly agreed that they know of no one
more deserving of their love and honor? . . .
Now do listen to my paternal admonitions;
correct this fault, be a little more humble and
modest, think better of your friends, and submit to their judgment—trust your own only
so far as it agrees with theirs. You will certainly be rewarded for this improvement in
your conduct by a notable increase of tranquillity and cheerfulness in your view both of
the past and of the future; and in the hope
that you will be buxom and good, I conclude
my New Year's lecture. . . .

SAMUEL JOHNSON TO MRS. THRALE.

London, November 13, 1783.

Since you have written to me with the attention and tenderness of olden time, your

letters give me a great part of the pleasure which a life of solitude admits. You will never bestow any share of your good-will on one who deserves better. Those that have loved longest love best. A sudden blaze of kindness may by a single blast of coldness be extinguished; but that fondness that length of time has connected with many circumstances and occasions, though it may for a while be depressed by disgust or resentment, with or without a cause, is hourly revived by accidental recollection. To those that have lived long together, every thing heard and every thing seen recalls some pleasure communicated or some benefit conferred, some petty quarrel or some slight endearment. Esteem of great powers, or amiable qualities newly discovered, may embroider a day or a week, but a friendship of twenty years is interwoven with the texture of life. A friend may be often found and lost; but an *old friend* never can be found, and nature has provided that he cannot easily be lost. . . .

GEORGE ELIOT TO MADAME BODICHON.

WITLEY, October 15, 1878.

The days pass by without my finding time to tell you what I want to tell you. How delighted I was to have a good account of you! But every bright day, and we have had many such, has made me think the more of you, and hope that you were drawing in strength from the clear, sweet air. I miss so much the hope that I used always to have of seeing you in London, and talking over everything just as we used to do—in the way that will never exactly come with any one else. How unspeakably the lengthening of memories in common endears our old friends! The new are comparatively foreigners, with whom one's talk is hemmed in by mutual ignorance. The one cannot express, the other cannot divine. . . .

CHARLES LAMB TO WILLIAM WORDSWORTH.

LONDON, August 9, 1815.

. . . Our panegyrist * I thought had forgotten one of the objects of his youthful admiration; but I was agreeably removed from that scruple by the laundress knocking at my door this morning, almost before I was up, with a present of fruit from my young friend, etc. There is something inexpressibly pleasant to me in these *presents*, be it fruit, or fowl, or

* Talfourd

brawn, or *what not.* Books are a legitimate
cause of acceptance. If presents be not the
soul of friendship, undoubtedly they are the
most spiritual part of the body of that intercourse. There is too much narrowness of
thinking in this point. The punctilio of acceptance, methinks, is too confined and strait-
laced. I could be content to receive money,
or clothes, or a joint of meat from a friend.
Why should he not send me a dinner as well as
a dessert? I would taste him in the beasts of
the field and through all creation. Therefore
did the basket of fruit of the juvenile Talfourd
not displease me; not that I have any thoughts
of bartering or reciprocating these things. To
send him any thing in return would be to reflect suspicion of mercenariness upon what I
know he meant a free-will offering. Let him
overcome me in bounty. In this strife a generous nature loves to be overcome. . . .

———

CHARLES DICKENS TO CLARKSON STANFIELD.

TAVISTOCK HOUSE, Friday Night,
November 3, 1854.

First of all, here is enclosed a letter for Mrs.
Stanfield, which, if you don't immediately and
Vol. I.

faithfully deliver, you will hear of in an un-
pleasant way from the station-house at the
curve of the hill above you.

Secondly, this is not to remind you that we
meet at the Athenæum next Monday at five,
because none but a mouldy swab as never
broke biscuit or lay out on the for'sel-yardarm
in a gale of wind ever forgot an appointment
with a messmate.

But what I want you to think of at your
leisure is this : When our dear old Macready
was in town last, I saw it would give him so
much interest and pleasure if I promised to go
down and read my " Christmas Carol " to the
little Sherborne Institution, which is now one
of the few active objects he has in the life
about him, that I came out with that promise
in a bold—I may say a swaggering way. Consequently, on Wednesday, the 20th of December, I am going down to see him, with Kate
and Georgina, returning to town in good time
for Christmas, on Saturday, the 23d. Do you
think you could manage to go and return with
us ? I really believe there is scarcely any thing
in the world that would give him such extraordinary pleasure as such a visit, and if you

would empower me to send him an intimation that he may expect it, he will have a daily joy in looking forward to the time (I am seriously sure) which we—whose light has not gone out, and who are among our old dear pursuits and associations—can scarcely estimate.

I don't like to broach the idea in a careless way, and so I propose it thus, and ask you to think of it.

CHARLES DICKENS TO WILKIE COLLINS.

GAD'S HILL PLACE, HIGHAM-BY-ROCHESTER, KENT,
Tuesday Night, October 14, 1862.

Frank Beard has been here this evening—of course since I posted my this day's letter to you, and has told me that you are not at all well, and how he has given you something which he hopes and believes will bring you round. It is not to convey this insignificant piece of intelligence, or to tell you how anxious I am that you should come up with a wet sheet and a flowing sail (as we say at sea when we are not sick) that I write. It is simply to say what follows, which I hope may save you some mental uneasiness. For I was stricken ill when I was doing "Bleak House," and I shall not easily forget what I suffered under the fear of not being able to come up to time.

Dismiss that fear (if you have it) altogether from your mind. Write to me at Paris at any moment, and say you are unequal to your work and want me, and I will come to London straight and do your work. I am quite confident that, with your notes and a few words of explanation, I could take it up at any time and do it. Absurdly unnecessary to say that it would be a makeshift! But I could do it at a pinch, so like you as that no one should find out the difference. Don't make much of this offer in your mind; it is nothing, except to ease it. If you should want help, I am as safe as the bank. The trouble would be nothing to me, and the triumph of overcoming the difficulty great. Think it a Christmas number, an "Idle Apprentice," a "Lighthouse," a "Frozen Deep." I am as ready as in any of these cases to strike in and hammer the hot iron out.

You won't want me. You will be well (and thankless!) in no time. But there I am; and I hope that the knowledge may be a comfort to you. Call me, and I come.

As Beard always has a sense of medical

responsibility, and says any thing important about a patient in confidence, I have merely remarked here that "Wilkie" is out of sorts. Charley (who is here with Katie) has no other cue from me.

———

LADY HOLLAND TO FRANCIS HORNER.

HOLLAND HOUSE, October 1, 1816.

I am glad *my doctors* send you from the keen air of your native mountains ; it must be insufferable, but they will not mend the matter by sending you into London. I accordingly trust to your docility, and your sister's good nature, in expecting you to drive from Barnet straight here, where you will occupy three south rooms, regulated as Allen shall direct, and have your hours, and company, and occupations entirely at your own disposal. Such books and papers as you may require can easily be brought from your own house. Remember your own house is in the heart of London, your sitting and bedroom exposed to the *east ;* that, with your facility to all who ever pretend from acquaintance to friendship, you cannot be denied at your door ; that the calm, which is so necessary to you, will be perpetually broken in upon.

These three rooms open into each other, and are perfectly warm; your servant will sleep close to you, and your sister will have a room adjoining to this apartment. Pray spare me all the commonplace compliments of giving trouble, and taking up too many rooms. What you know I feel towards you ought to exempt me from any such trash. From henceforward till June, when I look forward to a thorough amendment, you must lay your account to have me, heart, soul, and time, entirely devoted to your welfare and comfort; and I am satisfied in this, because Allen says it is right. I am afraid your sister may think it a bad exchange, from living solely with you, to come amongst strangers; but tell her I already feel warmth towards her for her affectionate intention of nursing you, and that I will try and make her residence as little irksome as possible. Do, my dear friend, yield to my entreaties. . . .

RICHARD BROCKLESBY TO EDMUND BURKE.

LONDON, July 2, 1788.

My veneration of your public conduct for many years past, and my real affection for your private virtues and transcendent worth, made

me yesterday take a liberty with you, in a moment's conversation at my house, to make you
an instant present of £1,000, which for years
past, by will, I had destined, as a testimony of
my regard, on my decease.

This you modestly desired me not to think
of ; but I told you what I now repeat, that,
unfavored as I have lived a long life, unnoticed
professionally by any party of men, and though
unknown at court, I am rich enough to spare
to virtue (what others waste in vice) the above
sum, and still reserve an annual income greater
than I spend. I shall receive, at the India
House, a bill I have discounted for £1,000 on
the fourth of next month, and then shall be
happy that you will accept this proof of my
sincere love and esteem ; and, let me add, " Si
res ampla domi similisque affectibus esset," I
should be happy to repeat the like every year,
until I saw your merit rewarded as it ought to
be at court.

That you may long live, for talents an ornament to human kind, and for your country,
your friends, and family, the same happy man
in prosperity, as you have approved yourself
whilst withdrawn from the sunshine of a court,

—this, with much more (if any thing can be better), is the fervent wish of, my dear Burke, your sincere and ever affectionate humble servant.

———

EDMUND BURKE TO RICHARD BROCKLESBY.

LONDON, July 17, 1788.

You wished me to return you only a verbal answer to the letter of extraordinary kindness which you left upon my table in Gerard Street, when I was last in town. In truth, it is hard to give it any proper answer, either verbally or in writing, or to express in any way the sense I have of your friendship. That friendship has commenced many years since, and continued without intermission to this hour, by a series of good offices on your part, without any power of returning them on mine. But you are kind enough not only to pass by all this, but to take for merit the cause of my incapacity to make any kind of return for the services I receive of all descriptions. I am under no apprehension from writing this, or from letting you know that I consider your steady and deliberate good opinion of me as a real honor to me, and to the principles we entertain in common. You have thought of me in your will; but you choose to anticipate the legal period and the natural, and to give me my legacy when my receiving it can be mixed with no regret. You tell me, too, that it will prove of no inconvenience to yourself, or those you mean to succeed to you,— the only conditions upon which I would consent to profit of an earlier or later will. Your delicacy would prevent you from receiving this acknowledgment of your living legacy under my hand. But it becomes me to leave that testimony in your power to preserve or destroy it, at your pleasure, not at mine. Indeed, my dear friend, I shall never be ashamed to have it known that I am obliged to one who never can be capable of converting his kindness into a burthen, nor to profess how sincerely and unalterably I am, my dear Doctor, your most affectionate and faithful humble servant.

ROBERT SOUTHEY TO JOSEPH COTTLE.

GRETA HALL, April 28, 1808.

What you say of my copy-rights affects me very much. Dear Cottle, set your heart at rest on that subject. It ought to be at rest. They were yours; fairly bought, and fairly sold. You bought them on the chance of their success, what no London bookseller would have done; and had they not been bought, they could not have been published at all. Nay, if you had not published " Joan of Arc," the poem never would have existed, nor should I, in all probability, ever have obtained that reputation which is the capital on which I subsist, nor that power which enables me to support it.

But this is not all. Do you suppose, Cottle, that I have forgotten those true and most essential acts of friendship which you showed me when I stood most in need of them? Your house was my house when I had no other. The very money with which I bought my wedding ring, and paid my marriage fees, was supplied by you. It was with your sisters that I left my Edith, during my six months' absence; and for the six months after my return, it was from you that I received, week by week, the little on which we lived, till I was enabled to live by other means. It is not the settling of our cash account that can cancel obligations like these. You are in the habit of preserving your letters, and if you were not, *I would entreat you to preserve this, that it might be seen hereafter*. Sure I am, that there was never a more generous, nor a kinder heart than yours, and you will believe me when I add that there does not live that man upon earth, whom I remember with more gratitude and more affection. My heart throbs, and my eyes burn with these recollections. Good night, my dear old friend and benefactor.

EDWARD GIBBON TO GEORGE DEYVERDUN.

LONDON, May 20, 1783.

How I love the sweet and free communication of our reciprocal feelings! We love each other during distance and silence, and we find it mutually sufficient to hear from time to time news of each other's health and welfare. To-day I want to write to you, and I begin without reproaches or apologies, as if we were about to resume the familiar conversation of yesterday.
. . . Lausanne had my first-fruits; it will always be endeared to me by the sweet recollections of my youth. After thirty years I recall to mind the young rakes who are now judges, the little maidens of the "Spring" society, who are now become grandmothers. Your country is delightful, and in spite of Jean

Jacques Rousseau's disgust, the manners and genius of its inhabitants appear to me to be well suited to the banks of the Lake of Leman. But there is a treasure which I could find only at Lausanne; which is a friend who agrees with me in ideas and feelings, and with whom I have never experienced a moment of tedium, coolness, or reserve. Formerly, in the freedom of mutual communications, we formed a hundred times the design of living together, and a hundred times have we decked it in all the details of romance, with a warmth that has astonished even ourselves. At present he dwells, or rather *you* dwell (for I am tired of this studied style), in a convenient and delightful house; I can see from hence my apartment, our common parlors, our table, our walks; but this marriage will be useless unless it is equally convenient to both the espoused, and I am sensible how many local circumstances, new tastes, and fresh connections may stand in the way of the fulfilment of those designs, which appear to us, in the distance, most agreeable. To settle my ideas, and to prevent our after regrets, you must disclose to me, with the frankness of which I have given you the example, the exter-

nal and internal picture of George Deyverdun.
My affection is too delicate to bear indifference and cold respect, and I should be ashamed
of a happiness for which I should be indebted,
not to my friend's inclination, but to his
fidelity. . . .

———

EDWARD GIBBON TO LADY SHEFFIELD.

LAUSANNE, October 22, 1784.

. . . My present life wants no foil, and shines
by its own native light. . . . An excellent house,
a good table, a pleasant garden, are no con-
temptible ingredients in human happiness.
The general style of society hits my fancy; I
have cultivated a large and agreeable circle of
acquaintance, and I am much deceived if I have
not laid the foundations of two or three more
intimate and valuable connections; but their
names would be indifferent, and it would require pages, or rather volumes, to describe
their persons and characters. With regard to
my standing dish, my domestic friend, I could
not be much disappointed, after an intimacy of
eight and twenty years. His heart and his
head are excellent; he has the warmest attachment for me, he is satisfied that I have the

same for him; some slight imperfections must be mutually supported; two bachelors, who have lived so long alone and independent, have their peculiar fancies and humors, and when the mask of form and ceremony is laid aside, every moment in a family life has not the sweetness of the honeymoon, even between the husbands and wives who have the truest and most tender regard for each other. Should you be very much surprised to hear of my being married? Amazing as it may seem, I do assure you that the event is less improbable than it would have appeared to myself a twelvemonth ago. Deyverdun and I have often agreed, in jest and in earnest, that a house like ours would be regulated, and graced, and enlivened, by an agreeable female companion; but each of us seems desirous that his friend should sacrifice himself for the public good. Since my residence here I have lived much in women's company; and, to your credit be it spoken, I like you the better the more I see of you. Not that I am in love with any particular person. I have discovered about half a dozen *wives* who would please me in different ways, and by various merits: one as a mistress (a widow, vastly like *the* Eliza: If she returns I am to bring them together); a second, a lively entertaining acquaintance; a third, a sincere good-natured friend; a fourth, who would represent with grace and dignity at the head of my table and family; a fifth, an excellent economist and housekeeper; and a sixth, a very useful nurse. Could I find all these qualities united in a single person, I should dare to make my addresses, and should deserve to be refused. . . .

GEORGE ELIOT TO MISS SARA HENNELL.

LONDON, August 21, 1852.

If there is any change in my affection for you it is that I love you more than ever, not less. I have as perfect a friendship for you as my imperfect nature can feel—a friendship in which deep respect and admiration are sweetened by a sort of flesh-and-blood sisterly feeling, and the happy consciousness that I have your affection, however undeservedly, in return. I have confidence that this friendship can never be shaken; that it must last while I last, and that the supposition of its ever being weakened by a momentary irritation is too contemptibly absurd for me to take the trouble to deny it. As

to your whole conduct to me, from the first
day I knew you, it has been so generous and
sympathetic that, if I did not heartily love
you, I should feel deep gratitude—but love ex-
cludes gratitude. It is impossible that I should
ever love two women better than I love you
and Cara. Indeed, it seems to me that I can
never love any so well ; and it is certain that I
can never have any friend—not even a husband
—who would supply the loss of those associations with the past which belong to you. Do
believe in my love for you, and that it will remain as long as I have my senses, because it is
interwoven with my best nature, and is depend-
ent, not on any accidents of manner, but on
long experience, which has confirmed the instinctive attraction of earlier days. . . .

———

NORMAN MACLEOD TO CHARLES KINGSLEY.

ADELAIDE PLACE, April 10, 1867.

When I wish to remember a friend daily I
don't answer his letter for days when it demands an immediate reply. What a presence
he becomes, and how humble and ashamed one
feels before him, especially when we have no
excuse for our silence which can bear his scru-

tiny. By this sinful process, "How often hath my spirit turned to thee?" ever since I received your note. I shall leave it to my boys that they may, when I am gone, learn from it that one so great and good gave their old dad so hearty and firm a grasp of his hand. God bless you for it! With all my heart I return it, for all you are and "a' Glencairn has been to me." I send my "plan," as a Highland laird termed his wife's likeness, to your lady, proud that it may find a humble place in her collection. The only inscription I am inclined to write on it would be Eccles. ii., 15, last clause.*

MRS. THOMAS CARLYLE TO MRS. STIRLING.

CHELSEA, October 21, 1859.

You dear, nice woman! there you are! a bright, cheering apparition to surprise one on a foggy October morning, over one's breakfast— that most trying institution for people who are "nervous" and "don't sleep!" . . .

Blessed be the inventor of photography! I set him above even the inventor of chloroform! It has given more positive pleasure to poor, suffering humanity than any thing that has

* "Then I said in my heart that this also is vanity."

"cast up " in my time or is like to—this art by
which even the " poor " can possess themselves
of tolerable likenesses of their absent dear ones.
And must n't it be acting favorably on the
morality of the country? I assure you I have
often gone into my own room, in the devil's own
humor—ready to swear at " things in general,"
and some things in particular—and, my eyes
resting by chance on one of my photographs of
long-ago places or people, a crowd of sad,
gentle thoughts has rushed into my heart, and
driven the devil out, as clean as ever so much
holy water and priestly exorcisms could have
done! I have a photograph of Haddington
church tower, and my father's tombstone in it
—of every place I ever lived at as a home—photographs of old lovers! old friends, old servants,
old dogs! In a day or two, you, dear, will be
framed and hung up among the " friends."
And that big, bright, kind, indomitable face of
yours will not be the least efficacious face there
for exorcising my devil, when I have him!
Thank you a thousand times for keeping your
word! Of course you would—that is just the
beauty of you, that you never deceive nor
disappoint.

ROBERT BURNS TO ROBERT AINSLIE.

MAUCHLINE, July 23, 1787.

There is one thing for which I set great store by you as a friend, and it is this—that I have not a friend upon earth, besides yourself, to whom I can talk nonsense without forfeiting some degree of his esteem. Now to one like me, who never cares for speaking any thing else but nonsense, such a friend as you is an invaluable treasure. I was never a rogue, but have been a fool all my life; and, in spite of all my endeavors, I see now plainly that I shall never be wise. Now it rejoices my heart to have met with such a fellow as you, who, though you are not just such a hopeless fool as I, yet I trust you will never listen so much to the temptations of the devil as to grow so very wise that you will in the least disrespect an honest fellow because he is a fool. In short, I have set you down as the staff of my old age, when the whole list of my friends will, after a decent share of pity, have forgot me.

Though in the morn comes sturt and strife,
    Yet joy may come at noon;
And I hope to live a merry, merry life,
    When a' thir days are done.

Write me soon, were it but a few lines just to tell me how that good, sagacious man, your father, is—that kind, dainty body, your mother —that strapping chiel, your brother Douglas— and my friend Rachel, who is as far before Rachel of old, as she was before her blear-eyed sister Leah.

————

LEIGH HUNT TO J. F.*

WIMBLEDON, July 4, 1846.

. . . I cannot express the pleasure your letter has given me.   I do not think you at all "wild" at Wimbledon, except inasmuch as a man ought to be, were it for nothing but the sake of so pleasant an alliteration.   I think you immensely reasonable and *cultivated* at Wimbledon, and rejoice to have found at the core of all your other qualities the true *inn*-ward light.

Seriously, I cannot overrate the comfort these meetings have given me, crowned and completed as it is with your own enjoyment of them. When I find myself in the little room, with the window open, and the garden before us, and a glass of claret on the table, care seems excluded; or, at least, if the sigh will come, I am surprised

* Presumably John Forster.

afterwards to think how briefly it stayed—how
I contrived to shut it out again, as I would an
east wind. We then surely want no one besides
ourselves. And yet, if you mention ——, why,
then indeed it is adding satisfaction to satisfaction; and I shall think of us three a hundred
times between this and to-morrow. . . .

JOHN LOCKE TO PHILIP VAN LIMBORCH.

ROTTERDAM, February 16, 1688.

. . . How I long to spend just an hour or
two, if no longer time were possible, with you!
To see, to hear, to embrace one's friends, is a
priceless joy to me. Our affection for one another needs no proof, and it could not be in-
creased by the ceremony of a farewell; yet I do
wish I could once more shake you by the hand,
once more assure you by word of mouth that I
am altogether yours. Many things tempt me
home again—the urgency of my friends in England, the necessity of looking after my own
neglected affairs, and other matters. But in
going away I almost feel as though I were
leaving my own country and my own kinsfolk;
for every thing that belongs to kinship, good-
will, love, kindness—every thing that binds

men together with ties stronger than the ties
of blood—I have found among you in abundance. I leave behind me friends whom I can
never forget, and I shall never cease to wish for
an opportunity of coming back to enjoy once
more the genuine fellowship of men who have
been such friends that, while far away from my
own connections, while suffering in every other
way, I have never felt sick at heart. As for
you, you best of men, most dearly and most
worthily beloved, when I think of your learning, your wisdom, your kindness, and candor
and gentleness, I seem to have found in your
friendship alone enough to make me always
rejoice that I was forced to pass so many years
among you. I know not how such a large portion of my life could elsewhere have been spent
more pleasantly, certainly it could not have
been spent more profitably. God give you
heaped-up happiness, protect your country and
your household, and enable you to go on in
your good work for your church and all good
men! To your excellent wife and to your
children, to the Veens and the Guenellons, and
all the rest, give my kindest good wishes and
my heartiest thanks for all the services they

have rendered me. Embrace them for me, and tell them I can never forget them, or their many, many proofs of unselfish affection. Farewell, most cherished of friends, and again, farewell

———

WILLIAM COWPER TO LADY HESKETH.

OLNEY, October 12, 1785.

It is no new thing with you to give pleasure ; but I will venture to say that you do not often give more than you gave me this morning. When I came down to breakfast, and found upon the table a letter franked by my uncle, and when opening that frank I found that it contained a letter from you, I said within myself : " This is just as it should be. We are all grown young again, and the days that I thought I should see no more are actually returned." You perceive, therefore, that you judged well when you conjectured that a line from you would not be disagreeable to me. It could not be otherwise than, as in fact it proved, a most agreeable surprise, for I can truly boast of an affection for you, that neither years nor interrupted intercourse have at all abated. I need only recollect how much I valued you once, and with how much cause, immediately to feel

a revival of the same value ; if that can be said
to revive, which at the most has only been dor-
mant for want of employment; but I slander it
when I say that it has slept.   A thousand times
have I recollected a thousand scenes, in which
our two selves have formed the whole of the
drama, with the greatest pleasure ; at times, too,
when I had no reason to suppose that I should
ever hear from you again.   I have laughed with
you at the "Arabian Nights Entertainment,"
which afforded us, as you well know, a fund of
merriment that deserves never to be forgot.   I
have walked with you to Netley Abbey, and
have scrambled with you over hedges in every
direction, and many other feats we have performed together, upon the field of my remembrance, and all within these few years.   Should
I say within this twelvemonth, I should not
transgress the truth.   The hours that I have
spent with you were among the pleasantest
of my former days, and are therefore chronicled
in my mind so deeply as to feel no erasure. . . .

WILLIAM COWPER TO LADY HESKETH.

OLNEY, February 9, 1786.

. . . And now, my dear, let me tell you once
more, that your kindness in promising us a visit

has charmed us both. I shall see you again.
I shall hear your voice. We shall take walks
together. I will show you my prospects, the
hovel, the alcove, the Ouse, and its banks—every
thing that I have described. I anticipate the
pleasure of those days not very far distant, and
feel a part of it at this moment. Talk not of
an inn! Mention it not for your life! We have
never had so many visitors, but we could easily
accommodate them all; though we have received Unwin, and his wife, and his sister, and
his son all at once. My dear, I will not let you
come till the end of May, or beginning of June,
because before that time my green-house will
not be ready to receive us, and it is the only
pleasant room belonging to us. When the
plants go out, we go in. I line it with mats
and spread the floor with mats; and there you
shall sit with a bed of mignonette at your side,
and a hedge of honeysuckles, roses, and jasmine; and I will make you a bouquet of myr-
tle every day. Sooner than the time I mention
the country will not be in complete beauty.
And I will tell you what you shall find at your
first entrance. Imprimis, as soon as you have
entered the vestibule, if you cast a look on

either side of you, you shall see on the right
hand a box of my making. It is the box in
which have been lodged all my hares, and in
which lodges Puss at present: but he, poor
fellow, is worn out with age, and promises to
die before you can see him. On the right hand
stands a cupboard, the work of the same author;
it was once a dove-cage, but I transformed it.
Opposite to you stands a table, which I also
made ; but a merciless servant having scrubbed
it until it became paralytic, it serves no purpose
now but of ornament ; and all my clean shoes
stand under it. On the left hand, at the farther
end of this superb vestibule, you will find the
door of the parlor, into which I will conduct
you, and where I will introduce you to Mrs.
Unwin, unless we should meet her before, and
where we will be as happy as the day is long.
Order yourself, my cousin, to the Swan at
Newport, and there you shall find me ready to
conduct you to Olney.

My dear, I have told Homer what you say
about casks and urns, and have asked him
whether he is sure that it is a cask in which
Jupiter keeps his wine. He swears that it is a
cask, and that it will never be any thing better
than a cask to eternity. So if the god is con-

tent with it, we must even wonder at his taste, and be so too.

<hr />

WILLIAM COWPER TO LADY HESKETH.

OLNEY, May 15, 1786.

From this very morning I begin to date the last month of our long separation, and confidently hope that before the fifteenth of June shall present itself, we shall have seen each other. Is it not so? And will it not be one of the most extraordinary eras of my extraordinary life? A year ago, we neither corresponded nor expected to meet in this world.

Wherefore is it (canst thou tell me?) that together with all those delightful sensations, to which the sight of a long-absent dear friend gives birth, there is a mixture of something painful: flutterings, and tumults, and I know not what accompaniments of our pleasure, that are in fact perfectly foreign from the occasion? Such I feel when I think of our meeting; and such I suppose feel you; and the nearer the crisis approaches, the more I am sensible of them. I know beforehand that they will increase with every turn of the wheels that shall convey me to Newport, when I shall set out to meet you; and that when we actually meet, the pleasure, and this unaccountable pain together, will be as much as I shall be able to support. I am utterly at a loss for the cause, and can only resolve it into that appointment by which it has been foreordained that all human delight shall be qualified and mingled with their contraries. For there is nothing formidable in you. To me at least there is nothing such, no, not even in your menaces, unless when you threaten me to write no more. Nay I verily believe, did I not know you to be what you are, and had less affection for you than I have, I should have fewer of these emotions, of which I would have none if I could help it. . . . You will tremble as you draw near to Newport, and so shall I; but we will both recollect that there is no reason why we should, and this recollection will at least have some little effect in our favor. We will likewise both take the comfort of what we know to be true, that the tumult will soon cease, and the pleasure long survive the pain, even as long I trust as we ourselves shall survive it. . . .

WILLIAM COWPER TO LADY HESKETH.

OLNEY, May 29, 1786.

Thou dear, comfortable cousin, whose letters, among all that I receive, have this property peculiarly their own, that I expect them without trembling, and never find any thing in them that does not give me pleasure; for which therefore I would take nothing in exchange that the world could give me, save and except that for which I must exchange them soon (and happy shall I be to do so), your own company. That, indeed, is delayed a little too long; to my impatience at least it seems so, who find the spring, backward as it is, too forward, because many of its beauties will have faded before you will have an opportunity to see them. We took our customary walk yesterday in the wilderness at Weston, and saw, with regret, the laburnums, syringas, and guelder-roses, some of them blown, and others just upon the point of blowing, and could not help observing—all these will be done before Lady Hesketh comes! Still, however, there will be roses, and jasmine, and honeysuckle, shady walks, and cool alcoves, and you will partake them with us. But I want you to have a share of every thing that is delightful here, and cannot bear that the advance of the season should steal away a single pleasure before you can come to enjoy it.

Every day I think of you, almost all the day

long; I will venture to say that even you were never so expected in your life. I called last week at the Quaker's to see the furniture of your bed, the fame of which had reached me. It is, I assure you, superb—of printed cotton, and the subject classical. Every morning you open your eyes on Phæton kneeling to Apollo, and imploring his father to grant him the conduct of his chariot for a day. May your sleep be as sound as your bed will be sumptuous, and your nights at least will be well provided for.

I shall send up the sixth and seventh books of the Iliad shortly, and shall address them to you. You will forward them to the General. I long to show you my workshop, and to see you sitting on the opposite side of the table. We shall be as close packed as two wax figures in an old-fashioned picture frame. I am writing in it now. It is the place in which I fabricate all my verse in summer-time. I rose an hour sooner than usual this morning, that I might finish my sheet before breakfast, for I must write this day to the General.

The grass under my windows is all bespangled with dewdrops, and the birds are singing in the apple trees, among the blossoms. Never poet had a more commodious oratory in which to invoke his Muse.

I have made your heart ache too often, my poor dear cousin, with talking about my fits of dejection. Something has happened that has led me to the subject, or I would have mentioned them more sparingly. Do not suppose, or suspect, that I treat you with reserve. There is nothing in which I am concerned that you shall not be made acquainted with. But the tale is too long for a letter. I will only add for your present satisfaction that the cause is not exterior, that it is not within the reach of human aid, and that yet I have a hope, myself, and Mrs. Unwin a strong persuasion, of its removal. I am indeed even now, and have been for a considerable time, sensible of a change for the better, and expect, with good reason, a comfortable lift from you. Guess, then, my beloved cousin, with what wishes I look forward to the time of your arrival, from whose coming I promise myself not only pleasure, but peace of mind,—at least an additional share of it. At present it is an uncertain and transient guest with me ; but the joy with which I shall see and converse with you at Olney may perhaps make it an abiding one.

WILLIAM COWPER TO LADY HESKETH.

OLNEY, June 4, 1786.

Ah! my cousin, you begin already to fear and quake. What a hero am I, compared with you! I have no fears of *you;* on the contray, am as bold as a lion. I wish that your carriage were even now at the door. You should soon see with how much courage I would face you. But what cause have you for fear? Am I not your cousin, with whom you have wandered in the fields of Freemantle, and at Bevis's Mount? who used to read to you, laugh with you, till our sides have ached, at any thing or nothing? And am I in these respects at all altered? You will not find me so; but just as ready to laugh, and to wander, as you ever knew me. A cloud perhaps may come over me now and then, for a few hours, but from clouds I was never exempted. And are not you the identical cousin with whom I have performed all these feats? The very Harriet whom I saw, for the first time, at De Grey's in Norfolk Street? (It was on a Sunday, when you came with my uncle and aunt to drink tea there, and I had dined there, and was just going back to Westminster.) If these things are so, and I am sure that you cannot gainsay a syllable of them all, then this consequence follows: and I do not promise myself more pleasure from your company than I shall be sure to find. Then you are my cousin, in whom I always delighted, and in whom I doubt not that I shall delight even to my latest hour. But this wicked coach-maker has sunk my spirits. What a miserable thing it is to depend, in any degree, for the accomplishment of a wish, and that wish so fervent, on the punctuality of a creature who I suppose was never punctual in his life! Do tell him, my dear, in order to quicken him, that if he performs his promise, he shall make my coach when I want one, and that if he performs it not, I will most assuredly employ some other man. . . .

———

WILLIAM COWPER TO LADY HESKETH.

OLNEY, June 12, 1786.

I am neither young nor superannuated, yet am I a child. When I had read your letter I grumbled ; not at you, my dearest cousin, for you are in no fault, but at the whole generation of coach-makers, as you may suppose, and at yours in particular. I foresaw and foreknew that he would fail in his promise, and yet was disappointed; was, in truth, no more prepared for what I expected with so much reason, than if I had not at all expected it. I grumbled till we went to dinner, and at intervals till we had dined; and when dinner was over, with very little encouragement, I could actually have cried. And if I had, I should in truth have thought them tears as well bestowed as most that I have shed for many years. At first I numbered months, then weeks, then days, and was just beginning to number hours, and now I am thrown back to days again. My first speech was, after folding up your letter (for I will honestly tell you all), I am crazed with Mondays, Tuesdays, and Wednesdays and St. Alban's, and Totteridge, and Hadley. When is she to set out? When is she to be here? Do tell me, for, perhaps, you understand it better than I. Why, says Mrs. Unwin (with much more composure in her air than properly belonged to her, for she also had her feelings on the occasion), she sets out to-morrow se'nnight, and will be here on the Wednesday after. And who knows that? replied I; will the coach-maker be at all more punctual in repairing the old carriage than in making the

new one? For my part, I have no hope of seeing her this month; and if it be possible, I will
not think of it, lest I should be again disappointed. And to say the truth, my dear, though
hours have passed since thus I said, and I have
had time for cooler consideration, the suspicion
still sticks to me that more delays may happen. . . . When I awake in the night, I feel
my spirits the lighter because you are coming.
When I am not at Troy, I am either occupied
in the recollection of a thousand passages of
my past life, in which you were a partaker with
me, or conversing about you with Mrs. Unwin.
Thus my days and nights have been spent
principally ever since you determined upon
this journey, and especially, and almost without interruption from any other subject, since
the time of your journey has seemed near at
hand. . . .

WILLIAM COWPER TO WILLIAM UNWIN.

OLNEY, July 3, 1786.

After a long silence I begin again. A day
given to my friends is a day taken from Homer,
but to such an interruption now and then occur-
ring, I have no objection. Lady Hesketh is,
as you observe, arrived, and has been with us

near a fortnight. She pleases everybody, and is pleased in her turn with every thing she finds at Olney; is always cheerful and sweet-tempered, and knows no pleasure equal to that of communicating pleasure to us, and to all around her. This disposition in her is the more comfortable, because it is not the humor of the day, a sudden flash of benevolence and good spirits, occasioned merely by a change of scene; but it is her natural turn, and has governed all her conduct ever since I knew her first. We are consequently happy in her society, and shall be happier still to have you to partake with us in our joy. . . . I am fond of the sound of bells, but was never more pleased with those of Olney than when they rang her into her new habitation. It is a compliment that our performers upon these instruments have never paid to any other personage (Lord Dartmouth excepted) since we knew the town. In short, she is, as she ever was, my pride and my joy, and I am delighted with every thing that means to do her honor. Her first appearance was too much for me; my spirits, instead of being greatly raised, as I had inadvertently supposed they would be, broke down with me under the pressure of too much joy, and left me flat, or rather melancholy throughout the day, to a degree that was mortifying to myself and alarming to her. But I have made amends for this failure since, and in point of cheerfulness have far exceeded her expectations, for she knew that sable had been my suit for many years. . . .

FRANCIS JEFFREY TO CHARLES DICKENS.

CRAIGCROOK, July 27, 1849.

I have been very near dead, and am by no means sure that I shall *ever* recover from the malady which has confined me mostly to bed for the last five weeks, and which has only, within the last three days, allowed me to leave my room for a few hours in the morning. But I must tell you that, living or dying, I retain for you, unabated and unimpaired, the same cordial feelings of love, gratitude, and admiration, which have been part of my nature, and no small part of my pride and happiness, for the last twenty years. I could not let *another* number of your *public* benefactions appear, without some token of my private and peculiar thankfulness for the large share of gratification I receive from them all; and therefore I rise

from my couch and indite these few lines (the
second I have been able to make out in my
own hand since my illness), to explain why I
have not written before, and how little I am
changed in my feelings toward you by sickness
or a nearer prospect of mortality. I am better,
however, within these last days; and hope still
to see your bright eye, and clasp your open
hand, once more at least before the hour of
final separation. In the meantime you will be
glad, though I hope not surprised, to hear that
I have no acute suffering, no disturbing apprehensions or low spirits, but possess myself in a
fitting and indeed cheerful tranquillity, without
impatience or any unseemly anxiety as to the
issue I am appointed to abide.

With kindest and most affectionate remem-
brances to your true-hearted and affectionate
Kate, and all your blooming progeny, ever and
ever, my dear Dickens, affectionately yours.

HORACE WALPOLE TO GEORGE MONTAGU.

PARIS, November 21, 1765.

. . . My gout and my stick have entirely left
me. I totter still, it is true, but I trust shall be
able to whisk about at Strawberry as well almost

as ever. When that hour strikes, to be sure I
shall not be very sorry. The sameness of the
life here is worse than any thing but English
politics and the House of Commons. Indeed,
I have a mind still to see more people here,
more sights, and more of the Dumenil. The
Dauphin, who is not dead yet, detains the whole
court at Fontainebleau, whither I dare not venture, as the situation is very damp and the
lodgings abominable. Sights too, I have
scarce seen any yet, and I must satisfy my curiosity; for hither, I think, I shall never come
again. No, let us sit down quietly and com-
fortably, and enjoy our coming old age. Oh,
if you are in earnest, and will transplant yourself to Roehampton, how happy I shall be!
You know, if you believe an experience of above
thirty years, that you are one of the very, very
few for whom I really care a straw. You know
how long I have been vexed at seeing so little
of you. What has one to do, when one grows
tired of the world, as we both do, but to draw
nearer and nearer, and gently waste the remains
of life with the friends with whom one began
it! Young and happy people will have no
regard for us and our old stories, and they are

in the right; but we shall not tire one another; we shall laugh together when nobody is by to laugh at us, and we may think ourselves young enough when we see nobody younger. Roehampton is a delightful spot, at once cheerful and retired. You will amble in your chaise about Richmond Park; we shall see one another as often as we like; I shall frequently peep at London, and bring you tales of it, and we shall sometimes touch a card with the Clive,* and laugh our fill; for I must tell you I desire to die when I have nobody left to laugh with me. . . .

ALLAN CUNNINGHAM TO JAMES HOGG.

London, February 16, 1826.

It required neither present of book, nor friend, nor the recalling of old scenes, to render your letter a most welcome one. You are often present to my heart and fancy, for your genius and your friendliness have secured you a place in both. . . .

Often do I tread back to the foot of old Queensberry, and meet you coming down amid the sunny rain, as I did some twenty years ago.

* Kitty Clive, the actress, who for some time was a near neighbor of Walpole's.

The little sodded shealing where we sought shelter rises now on my sight; your two dogs (old Hector was one) lie at my feet; the "Lay of the Last Minstrel" is in my hand, for the first time, to be twice read over after sermon, as it really was; poetry, nothing but poetry, is our talk, and we are supremely happy. Or, I shift the scene to Thornhill, and there, while the glass goes round, and lads sing and lasses laugh, we turn our discourse on verse, and still our speech is song. Poetry had then a charm for us which has since been sobered down. I can now meditate without the fever of enthusiasm upon me; yet age to youth owes all or most of its happiest aspirations, and contents itself with purifying and completing the conceptions of early years.

We are both a little older and a little graver than we were some twenty years ago, when we walked in glory and joy on the side of old Queensberry. . . .

The evil news of Sir Walter's losses came on me like an invasion. I wish the world would do for him now what it will do in fifty years, when it puts up his statue in every town. Let it lay out its money in purchasing an estate, as the nation did to the Duke of Wellington, and money could never be laid out more worthily. . . .

———

THOMAS CARLYLE TO JAMES JOHNSTONE.

EDINBURGH, February 4, 1822.

. . . In fact, there are few events in my history that yield a more placid enjoyment to my mind than reading a letter from you or writing one for your perusal. In such cases the sober certainty of your many affectionate and faithful feelings towards me—not altogether unrequited, I hope—mingles itself with the happy recollection of many virtuous and cheerful hours that we have spent together long ago—before either of us had tasted *how* bitter a thing is worldly life ; and how wofully our young purposes were to be marred by the low impediment of this confused, inane, and noisy vortex into which both of us have been cast, and where we are still toiling, and striving, and jostling and being jostled, according to the sentence passed on Adam, and fulfilled on all his poor descendants. The moonshine nights during which we have strolled along the *loanings* of our native Annandale, the sunny days we have spent in basking on our own *braes*,—talking so copiously and heartily of all things that we knew or did not know ; those nights and days are " with the days beyond the Flood," we shall not see them more ; but the memory of them is still bright in the soul, and will make us recollect each other with pleasure even to the end. It is a rare fortune that gives to the man the friends of the boy, unsullied by unworthy actions, and still maintaining some similarity of tastes ; it is a happiness, however, which has been ours, and, I trust, will continue so always. Nor do I in the smallest abandon the hope that future days will be calmer than those that have passed and are passing over us. Depend upon it, my good friend, there is a time coming when, though we may not be great men, we shall be placid ones ; when, having mended by much toil what is capable of being mended in our condition, and resigned ourselves to endure with much patience what in it is incapable of mending, we shall meet together like toil-worn wayfarers descending the mountain cheerily and smoothly which we climbed with danger and distress. " We will laugh and sing and tell old tales," and forget that our lot has been hard, when we think that our hearts have been firm

and our conduct true and honest to the last.
This should console us whatever weather it is
with us : the task is brief ; and great is the
reward of doing it well. . . .

SAMUEL JOHNSON TO JAMES BOSWELL.

ASHBOURNE, September 1, 1777.

On Saturday I wrote a very short letter, immediately upon my arrival hither, to show you
that I am not less desirous of the interview than
yourself. Life admits of no delays : when pleasure can be had, it is fit to catch it : every hour
takes away part of the things that please us,
and, perhaps, part of our disposition to be
pleased. When I came to Lichfield, I found
my old friend, Harry Jackson, dead. It was a
loss, and a loss not to be repaired, as he was
one of the companions of my childhood. I
hope we may long continue to gain friends ;
but the friends which merit or usefulness can
procure us are not able to supply the place of
an old acquaintance, with whom the days of
youth may be retraced, and those images revived which gave the earliest delight. If you
and I live to be much older, we shall take great
delight in talking over the Hebridean journey.

In the meantime it may not be amiss to con-
trive some other little adventure, but what it
can be I know not; leave it, as Sidney says,

" To virtue, fortune, time, and woman's breast,"

for I believe Mrs. Boswell must have some part
in the consultation. . . .

CHARLES LAMB TO HENRY CRABB ROBINSON.

COLEBROOK ROW, ISLINGTON, January 20, 1826.

I called upon you this morning, and found
that you were gone to visit a dying friend. I
had been upon a like errand. Poor Norris . . .
in him I have a loss the world cannot make up.
He was my friend and my father's friend all
the life I can remember. I seem to have made
foolish friends ever since. Those are friendships
which outlive a second generation. Old as I
am waxing, in his eyes I was still the child he
first knew me. To the last he called me Charley.
I have none to call me Charley now. He was
the last link that bound me to the Temple.
You are but of yesterday. In him seem to
have died the old plainness of manners and
singleness of heart. Letters he knew nothing

of, nor did his reading extend beyond the pages of the *Gentleman's Magazine.* Yet there was a pride of literature about him from being amongst books (he was librarian), and from some scraps of doubtful Latin which he had picked up in his office of entering students, that gave him very diverting airs of pedantry. Can I forget the erudite look with which, when he had been in vain trying to make out a black-letter text of Chaucer in the Temple Library, he laid it down and told me that—"in these old books, Charley, there is sometimes a deal of very indifferent spelling,"—and seemed to console himself in the reflection! His jokes, for he had his jokes, are now ended; but they were old trusty perennials, staples that pleased after *decies repetita,* and were always as good as new. One song he had, which was reserved for the night of Christmas-day, which we always spent in the Temple. It was an old thing, and spoke of the flat bottoms of our foes and the possibility of their coming over in darkness, and alluded to threats of an invasion many years blown over; and when he came to the part

"We 'll still make 'em run, and we 'll still make 'em sweat,
   In spite of the devil and *Brussels Gazette!*"

his eyes would sparkle as with the freshness of
an impending event.   And what is the *Brussels
Gazette* now? I cry while I enumerate these
trifles. "How shall we tell them in a stranger's
ear?" . . .

———

BERNARD BARTON TO W. B. DONNE.

WOODBRIDGE, June 25 1847.

I send thee the annexed little tribute, not to
challenge any laud for its poetical merits, nor
because the character it commemorates had
much of what scholars and critics would call
poetical in his composition, but simply because
his had the *elements*, the material of such *in my
eye*. He was a hearty old yeoman of about
eighty-six—had occupied the farm in which he
lived and died about fifty-five years. Social,
hospitable, friendly; a liberal master to his
laborers, a kind neighbor, and a right merry
companion "within the limits of becoming
mirth." In politics, a staunch Whig; in his
theological creed, as sturdy a Dissenter; yet
with no more party spirit in him than a child.
He and I belonged to the same book club for
about forty years. He entered about fifteen
years before I came into these parts, and was
really a pillar in our literary temple.   Not that

he greatly cared about books, or was deeply read in them, but he loved to meet his neighbors, and get them round him, on any occasion, or no occasion at all. As a fine specimen of the true English yeoman, I have met few to equal, hardly any to surpass him, and he looked the character as well as he acted it till within a very few years, when the strong man was bowed by bodily infirmity. About twenty-six years ago, in his dress costume of a blue coat and yellow buckskins, a finer sample of John Bullism you would rarely see. It was the whole study of his long life to make the few who revolved round him in his little orbit as happy as he always seemed to be himself; yet I was gravely queried with when I happened to say that his children had asked me to write a few lines to his memory, whether I could do this in keeping with the general tone of my poetry. The speaker doubted if he was a decidedly pious character. He had at times, in his altitudes, been known to vociferate, at the top of his voice, a song of which the chorus was certainly not teetotalish:

> " Sing, old Rose, and burn the bellows,
> Drink and drive dull care away."

I would not deny the vocal impeachment, for I had heard him sing the song myself, though not for the last dozen years. As for his being or not being a decidedly pious character, that depended partly on who might be called on to decide the question. He was not a man of much profession, but he was a most diligent attender of his place of worship, a frequent and I believe a serious reader of his Bible, and kept an orderly and well-regulated house. In his blither moods I certainly have heard him sing that questionable ditty before referred to, but, as it appeared to me, not under vinous excitement so much as from an unforced hilarity which habitually found vent in that explosion ; and I think he never in my presence *volunteered* that song. It was pretty sure to be asked for once in a while, by some who liked to hear themselves join in the chorus. I believe it was his only one, with the exception of Watts's hymns, which he almost knew by heart, and sang on Sunday, at meeting, with equal fervor and unction. Take the good old man for all in all, I look not to see his like again, for the breed is going out, I fear. His fine spirit of humanity was better, methinks, than much of that which

apes the tone and assumes the form of divinity.
So now I think I have told thee enough to
weary thee, in prose, as well as verse, of my old
neighbor and friend, the Suffolk yeoman.

END OF VOL. I.